Tao Of Maceo
Identity, Relationships, Work: A Journal On Living

Maceo Paisley

Edited by Sundai Johnson
Cover art by Lorenzo Diggins Jr.
Back Cover Layout by Sophia Chang

Correspondence Print
454B Jung Jing Rd
Los Angeles, CA 90012

ISBN 978-0-9862828-4-3
Distriubuted by CBC Press in Los Angeles, CA
Library of Congress Cataloging-in-Publication Data

To Helen: Mom, you gave me an infinite
love and access to daily wisdom that
I continue to benefit from.

Sara,
Thanks for listening).

CHECKPOINTS

What Are We Doing Here?

I'm pretty sure the first thing I thought after being born was, "It's noisy out here." It used to just be my Mother's voice and my own. I probably couldn't even tell the difference between the two. Since I've left the womb I've noticed we're all running, back and forth, and sometimes, seems like it's for no reason. What we envision to be goodness and happiness has been passed down so many times, I wonder if they have lost their quality along this intergenerational game of telephone. I don't think Life is just about the materials we acquire, and the actions we perform but about the meaning we imbue those actions with. And, because we are all a little different, what is meaningful to us is subject to difference as well.

Through our identity, relationships, and work, we write the story of our lives and answer the age old question of "What are we doing here?" We know that the destination is the same for us all— for now, it is death— so how we get there is an important part of defining ourselves. I believe that we give ourselves the opportunity to die well, by living well. I want to have a clear idea of what 'living well' means and embrace all of my strengths and shortcomings along the way. Our bio is our bias, but by putting my ideals on paper I give myself a better vantage point to inspect them and know the difference between these, and the invisible influences that might lead me to live outside of my ideals. That's what the Tao Of Maceo is.

Every business has a mission or business plan, and every group has a motto or a values statement that helps them hold true to what they are. It was important to me that I write down a personal constitution, that I can refer back to when I fall off track or get distracted by the noise of the world. In Chinese *tao* or *dao* means t*he road, way, or path*. In Chinese philosophy the Tao is the natural order of the universe. I wanted to be clear on what my own path was, so

I began journaling privately and on social media, to share.

It's a helpful benchmark to be able to see where I've come from and have a guide post about how I want to get where I am going.

In some ways I view life like a Rubick's Cube: there are many ways to solve it, but in order to do so, you have to be willing to inspect all sides. Just like a Rubick's Cube, every solution is tied to a bunch of other solutions, so the holistic approach gives you access to greater understanding of what is going on. If life is like a Rubick's cube then this book is my algorithm for solving it my way. It might not be the same way you'd do it, but I encourage you, as a reader to find the difference you have from my understanding of things as a way to sharpen your own perception of the world.

Tao Of Maceo is a personal inventory, intended to put my views on paper so that I can have a better understanding of my fallacies, limiting beliefs, biases, and other notions that might inhibit me from being all that I can be. I am releasing this inventory to share my insights, tips and tricks, knowledge, perspectives, and whatever wisdom I have access to in the hopes that it might be of aid to others. My thoughts and perspectives are not entirely unique, but where my ideas are common they may provide some consolation to folks who might have otherwise felt alone.

I am an artist, not a self-help guru, but in my practice of art, I have learned a lot about myself and thus, a lot about Life. My hope is that "my two cents" contributes to a collective wisdom greater than the sum of its parts —an old wisdom that allows new wisdom to emerge from it. You may not find answers in this book, but instead a dialogue of, and with, the self, led by my personal inquiry.

I'm putting Tao Of Maceo into the world to be forthcoming with my ideas in such a way, that they stimulate deep inner conversation and inspire others to reflect on how they live. This in turn, might propel them to make adjustments in kind to be whole, healthy, and self-determinant.

You don't have to read this book in consecutive order. You don't have to read it at all! Treat it like a Rubick's Cube: pick it up and put it down. Play with this book, tear out pages and highlight sections that inspire your thoughts. Feel free to pop around to the different sections as needed. Since I am not a linear thinker, the topics follow groups but in no particular sequence.This is the book I think everyone should write in their own way, take stock of what ideas guide your living, inspect them, and if you feel they are valuable, share those ideas with the world. This is my call to action. Come for the pull quotes, stay for the philosophical diatribes on consciousness, grief and morality.

Love, Maceo

SELF

IDENTITY

Me, MySelf, and I

The first thing I'd like to convey is that I have multiple identities. No, I don't have Multiple Personality Disorder. I'm saying that my identity is comprised of conflicting and complementary traits that express themselves in response to various environmental conditions. Reason suggests that if everything that exists is a part of the universe, and I exist, then I am also part of the universe. Sensation however, would argue that my experiences are unique, and that causes a profound feeling of isolation that I am constantly overcoming. When I say that I am multiple personalities, I mean that I am both a body, whose material existence is fully dependant on the existence of everything else, a being, entirely alone in my experience of existing. I feel like different parts of identity form like Russian Matryoshka (stacking) dolls, where various elements of my personhood develop from pre-existing layers.

Consider how we understand aging. I look completely different than I did in my childhood. My values and tastes have also shifted, but I am still "me". **We are not made up of a fixed set of characteristics, but a responsive range of expressions** oriented around a primary set of ingredients. Every shade of our emotions and thoughts come from a basic ken, range of vision or understanding. This range shifts and expands as new layers of consciousness form, and beneath it all, is a core set of dispositions that are not immune to change, but resonate as True. If we think of our subconscious as one entire cognitive body all its own, it makes sense why we understand so little about it.

Subconscious is the oldest, most sensitive mind and sometimes, it isn't really able to, or interested in, sharing all its thoughts. Just as there are layers of truth, these layers also make up the divisions of identity that comprise us.

We keep secrets from ourselves.

Other times, the conscious mind is interrupted by these subconscious thoughts. The subconscious mind sits next to the soul within us. In doing so, all the universal wisdom that connects us to the stars and trees comes to us from the most basic energetic identity: the soul or conscience at the core of our being. Our next layer, the subconsciousness, can't speak directly to the whole universe to experience Truth. What we end up with is this crazy game of cosmic telephone where universal Truth has to pass through all these layers of consciousness and cognition before we can access it at the level we are operating on. These layers could be what is discussed when the Hindi talk about chakras. Computer scientists might understand these layers of consciousness as programming languages that may need intermediaries to relay the commands from the User to the Hardware. This view is generally where we end up with the mind/body duality, which is really like an energy/matter duality, or wave/particle duality, in particle physics where light is both wave and particle. To understand consciousness we have to talk about reality.

Reality. To put it simply, energy is the fundamental "stuff" of the whole universe. And as far as consciousness goes, it probably is more of a spectrum of consciousness than an on/off type of thing. Awareness is a relationship that requires at least two points.
1. You need the thing that IS aware, like a person or any thing that can focus attention.
2. You need the thing it is aware of. This second thing can be an object that is unable to be aware of stuff or it can be a thing that is capable of being aware of stuff, or finally, it can be the first thing looking back on itself (stuff = energy).

Ah! What's weird is the idea of self-awareness actually makes no sense because there has to be SOME separation between the *Looker* and the *Seer*, right? WRONG.

Since energy is everywhere, it is also everything. It can be both looker and seer simultaneously because even time is a product of energy. HOW SWAY!? Energy is so dope that it sees itself by manifesting in different states, it doesn't take on a constant form. There are different wavelengths, and currents, and phases that allow energy to fold back on itself, thus allowing it to be aware of its own changes.

Ok, so that brings us to matter. Matter is one of the states of energy that allow us, (we are also energy) to be more precise in our awareness. I guess Matter is like a product that Energy temporarily uses to track progress, like the hands of a clock, and movements in matter are what make time. So yea, matter is the clock that helps us measure time, but it's also a scale, a compass, and a thermometer, and so on. Matter is great for illustrating fluctuations in energy. Reality is the sum of all these fluctuations.

Humans fall within the spectrum of energy that allows us to engage with those fluctuations through our senses. Our senses allow us to perceive reality because they operate at the level of conscious that is most immediate for us to access. Arguably, there are several senses but there are 5 main ones that we are most familiar with. Reality isn't so much a simulation as some people say, in the sense that it is not connected to the changes in energy occurring beyond our senses. Reality is moreso a projection of energy into matter. Reality is like pure energy spread out as a bunch of checkpoints that Lookers can see. Lookers can't see everything at once, but they see just enough to inform their engagement with the energy around them. Reality is any of the conditions or arrangements that matter might take, to represent what's going on above, below, or otherwise, beyond the scope of energetic fluctuations we Lookers can perceive. To see more, we must keep moving and curiosity is one of the things that propels us to move.

Being curious can be troublesome in that we keep wanting to peel back the projection of reality to see more of what's behind it. Unfortunately where we fall on the spectrum of consciousness, at least in using only 5 senses, doesn't allow us to comprehend all that is going on beyond reality's projection. Reality itself is insufficient to inspect reality, there are limits to how much the Looker can see of themselves. We use logic, reason, theory, and emotion to explore possibility and deduction, calculation, and our imaginations help fill the gaps between what we can empirically observe and what seems consequentially evident.

Creativity is the the faculty that allows Lookers to move energy through work. It comes in imagination, analysis, synthesis, focus, abstraction, organization, bonding, expression, even reduction is an act of creativity. What we do with creativity gives us skills, tools, and technologies that amplify our perception and comprehension of energy fluctuations, thereby EXPANDING reality and sharpening its projection. Reality is not a simulation, it is a projection. What we can agree is real is not always a product of empirical certainty, but rather of shared experience. There is no objective, only the collective. As humans we are like water, in that we always have at least three states: being (soul), doing (body), and knowing (mind), engaging with reality at various layers of consciousness.

Flow. If reality is a projection then what are we doing? What are our bodies? I think I may have backed myself into a nihilistic ideological trap. If all of matter is only a projection of energy, then the energy flow must be what is behind the projection. In some sense this is true for me, but I still don't have access to direct energy flow because all energy flow happens on levels of consciousness that are not immediately available to me. My ability to move within the projection of reality is based on how I engage with what's around me.

Some economists talk about life as an equilibrium game, and I understand this metaphor to mean that if you want to continue playing the game, the first thing you have to do is grab the pieces and engage. The body is a game piece or the controller. In the physical world Matter matters because it is the container that holds the energy. Matter itself is energy expressed in a form that can be handled. Grab life by the matter.

Energy is like water, also comes in a few forms. One form is vapor, but we can't just drink the water vapor that is in the air. In liquid form, we can drink it to quench our thirst. Even a hard block of ice has to be chiseled down and melted in our mouths for it to be an effective thirst quencher. Water's usefulness is conditional: it's gotta be liquid. Since I have a physical body, I need to engage with energy on the level of consciousness that is physical, but there is still energy moving in me. Because I have a cognitive body (a mind) and other bodies, the better I get at connecting to those domains of consciousness, the better I know myself, and the more access I have to information and a greater sense of agency.

I grew up freestyle rapping. The whole point was to be so

intuitive, that you can make rhymes compose entire lyrical verses, on the spot. It was all about being so in tune with your message and the moment, that every word you said somehow contributed to the next moment and to the greater verse at large. If you got too caught up in the next word, you might overlook the arch of your verse and miss making punchlines. If you focus too much on the punchlines, your phrases don't make sense. Staying in flow is about being fully present in the moment but still having enough forethought to guide you in the direction you are trying to go. The same is pretty much true about any other improvisational practice, whether it be playing music, dancing, or comedy. The same is true for sports. You have to know where the goal is, but also stay focused on what is right in front of you. Being in flow requires processing several kinds of information at once, in a way that seems like supreme focus, but is truly as close to multitasking as it can get. Life is an improvisation.

When I am tapped in to all domains of consciousness, (mind, body, soul) New Age Spirituality might say, I am in alignment with myself, and my purpose. In flow, I am in harmony with all aspects of my identity and my environment—just as water is as much itself when it is a single drop, in a pool, a block of ice, or water vapor. I'm in a constant feedback loop, orienting and reorienting my self as conditions change, as I change, and as I change the conditions. Being in flow isn't just about tapping into the universal current, it is about fluidity of identity expression, and allows me to adapt my external conditions, yet maintain all that I am in Truth, whether that be pleasant or not. L**ife is not just about "going with the flow". We've got to recognize that we are PART OF the flow,** and be willing to use whatever agency, intuition, and expression we have to affect it.

I'm trash (Modesty). I'm the kind of person who looks through people's medicine cabinets. I might even Google the name of their prescrptions. I procrastinate, I'm selfish, I'm elitist, "bad at texting" , I'm trash. The Gospel of my religious upbringing tells me that *all have sinned and fall short of the glory of God*, (Romans 3:23). This is one of the ideas that has stuck with me my whole life. It says that no matter who you are, you are imperfect. Perfect is a word with a misunderstood history, coming from the latin words *per*— meaning "thorough, and completely", and *facere*— meaning "do". Loosely translated, things are perfect when they are complete. When a painter puts down their brush and looks at their work it is not perfect because there are no mistakes, it is perfect because it is finished. When I take this meaning and carry it over to my own life, it makes sense that any living person is imperfect,because their life is not finished. I see myself as a work in progress, being created, or co-created with my environment and experiences.

I am nowhere near perfect because my life is nowhere near complete. **A perfect life, comes only in death.** We speak so well of people after they have passed, even if we didn't necessarily like them all that much when they were alive, because they essentially have done all they can do. Looking back to Christianity, I see that our lives are full of mistakes, and the promise of Christianity is to enter heaven forgiven of all our sins as perfect beings. That is a wonderful idea, but while I'm here on Earth, it kind of sounds like we are all doomed to suffer for our mistakes.

At first this condemnation felt like a trick to guilt me into being modest, but after living a little bit, I realized that no matter how pure my intentions, or how much I practiced, I never actually made it to perfect. Fundamentally, that passage speaks to a truth "To err is human.", found in the poem, *An Essay on Criticism* by Alexander Pope. Not only am I trash, we all are. Being modest is nothing more than seeing yourself as small, or limited in ability, and if you've ever looked across the ocean you know it is true that we are all tiny in the grand scheme of things. In fact, we are vulnerable fragile beings that can't live more than a few minutes without air. Physically we are mortal beings, prone to harm and will all eventually die. Mentally and emotionally, we are very sensitive to fluctuations in mood and are also quite irrational and forgetful. It's important to me that I always remember "I could be wrong" when taking an opinion and be open to some degree of change. It is only with collaboration and support that we share agency and become better. We are not all-powerful, but we are all powerful.

An Aside:
My personal operating system works in such a way that I am always seeking to find what is capital 'T', *true*, in the highest sense. If I am operating from Truth, I know that the results of my actions and patterns are more reliable and this gives me peace and security. One thing I know about myself is that I am insecure, but not without reason. I am insecure, because the world is actually dangerous. My security comes from having a relatively firm grip on who I think I am, and what I think is going on in the world. As my picture of the world, and myself, sharpens, I get better and better at navigating it in ways that are true to me, or in other words, that honor my sense of self.

Now, back to perfection. Owning this revelation relieved the pressure to be perfect because I realize now, that it is impossible. The key is not to be perfect, but to make the most of my mistakes. Ideally, I would not make so many mistakes in the first place, but when I do, I have the chance to turn my lessons into blessings. Honestly, on my best days, I am 80% of the person I'd like to be. Even that conception of myself has flaws, so before we go any further let me just say. I am a sinner, or to put in secular language; I'm trash.

I'm amazing (Pride). Describing myself as trash is pretty extreme, but without admitting that I can be at fault, it becomes harder to realize when I am right. There has to be a compass that helps me gauge the difference between my virtues and vices — between *right* and *wrong*. Since I am naturally predisposed to insecurity, my default mechanism is to defend my self-image at all costs, whether I am correct or not. Based on the knowledge that I am not perfect, humility is knowledge of self. It helps me to have a more accurate self-image, granting me the agency to self-correct, and realign with what is True on more fundamental levels of experience. On the upside, any positive actions I take, or good I do in the world, is something to really celebrate as a product of grace — where the best parts of me shine through, in spite of my shortcomings.

I am not modest. Here I am writing a book that purports anyone actually cares about my thoughts and beliefs enough to spend some of their limited time here on Earth reading it. No, I am actually quite full of pride. Modesty is decreasing your projection of self-esteem or abilities. Being humble though, is not about suppressing my strengths but taking full ownership of my imperfections. It is about being just as forthcoming about my weaknesses as I am about my strengths, and recognizing and accepting the Truth of who I am. Humility is at the base of all goodness. Without an honest appraisal of who I am, I lose touch with my moral compass, as it becomes unclear what my motivations are.

The funny thing about virtues and vices is that they are not absolute, or unconditional. Contrary to popular opinion, pride is actually really good. If you have practiced a skill, and you are confident in your ability, pride that is rooted in an accurate appraisal of yourself is completely warranted. Also modesty isn't always good either. We sometimes shrink our abilities to avoid responsibility by "playing dumb" or appearing incapable. **Playing small is not humble, it is negligent.**

The other thing about vices, is that they can be complementary or contradictory. For example honesty and compassion are complementary. Without compassion, being brutally honest can lead to harming someone by weaponizing information about them in public or manipulating them. An example of contradictory virtues might be acceptance and optimism, because they can lead to inaction. For example, if you always accept the bad that comes in your life and look to for the bright side, you might miss the opportunities to make changes in your life that are right in front of you. It's hard to think of any part of myself as living in a vacuum because I live in a world that is so complex. I need to see the world through a few vantage points. Being really familiar with whatever tools I have at my disposal is my best bet for knowing which characteristics to lean into in a given moment. Morality is a skill. I practice assessing who I am, and using feedback from the results of my actions and those around me, to determine if my assessments are reflected as accurate.

Though I may be a sinner, I am proud and intelligent. I have forethought,I know how to have fun, I am a joyous person. For all these reasons and more, I am undeniably, amazing. Human beings are not perfect, but we are also not all bad. My identity and personhood are complex enough to hold contradicting notions together at once, which means that when I say "I'm trash" it's true, and when I say "I'm amazing" it is no less true. And by owning both equally, I get to claim my full potential.

Play. It is not just that I am trash and then immediately switch to being amazing. Often times I am a little bit of both. The world is not black and white. It makes sense that I would not be either. There must be some flexibility in understanding of myself as well as the world. When it comes to becoming a better person, it requires some free space to practice and fail with a sense of joy. Just as an artist has a studio to experiment and explore, creating places for play are crucial to the development of who I will be when it is time to show up in the world. Play is one of the most important parts of Life. Consequences of the things that happen in side of a game don't affect the conditions outside of the game. We have more freedom to explore who we might be in the absence of restriction within play. It allows us the safety to try and fail repeatedly without harming ourselves or causing harm to others.

When I was learning to do backflips I practiced on a pad, using a soft surface to cushion my body from potential accidents. Insulating myself from the consequences of my mistakes, both allowed me to develop confidence as my skills improved, and prevented me from becoming injured in training. There were foam pits to jump into, and padded blocks to jump off of— all allowing me to learn by exploring and failing repeatedly. I understood things were different outside of the container of play the first time I tried to do a wall flip on the street. I hit my head and scraped my elbow, and that pain was not only a lesson, but I had to take a break for a while to heal.

This is the importance of comfort, if gives your inner child a space to play, and I believe joy is the insulation that keeps my inner child safe. Play allows me to refill on confidence, and that confidence protects the beliefs I have about my ability to accomplish things. In this container of joy, play, and comfort, I get to jump as high as I want, throw paint on the canvas, or play drums really loudly and explore my limits without the consequence that comes with social reality. When we have the space to take full deep breaths and scream as loud as we can, we get the chance to know the extent of what our voice is capable of.

Exploring our fantasies and imagination helps us to see what we hold back when we engage with society. Whatsmore is that because play isn't really valuable to anyone else, it becomes sacred to us. We can do whatever we want and be curious without having to worry about pleasing others, we get to practice pleasing ourselves. The artists studio, and the play that occurs inside it, is not an indulgence but a necessity— a watering hole for joy and a replenishment of compassion.

Compassion for my imperfections gives me the courage to face them, and space to fortify them. When I have compassion for myself I am more equipped to be generous towards others, because I know that I am not all good, so I don't look down on others, or all bad, so I don't look down on myself. Through this trial and error behavior, and fulfilling our desires for ourselves, we need less from the world, and we have more to give. Compassion gives us room to be all that we are, and accept all that others are. It comes from joy, and joy comes from play. Don't let anyone steal your joy. If we can take the lessons we learn from play with us into other parts of our lives then play makes us better people.

Integrity. A lot of people talk about "living life to the fullest" as if it's all positive. If we take this phrase in truth it suggests that we embrace all of life's ups and downs. I believe that this is also how we should view ourselves. To live full lives, I imagine that we must be full people, embracing our strengths and weaknesses through humility. Balance and harmony become far more possible, because we let go of the need to maintain perfection and pleasantries. When I think of the word *integrity*, it meansholding the true shape of ourselves in the moral sense, just as we might use the word to describe an object that is very stable under physical pressure. For me, *integrity* speaks to the amount of strain, pressure, and external change that I can endure without having to compromise my shape.

Facing any fork in the road I ask myself, *Which path is most suitable for the kind of person I am, and will most likely lead me to becoming the person I want to be?* I don't think about pros and cons, I don't think about pain or pleasure I just try to gather as much information as possible and check that against everything I know about myself. The answer is usually pretty clearly tied to my purpose.

My favorite idea about purpose comes from a Japanese philosophy *Ikigai* which means *reason for being*. Now, I am not sure we are all necessarily endowed with one reason for being, but this framework certainly helps me make sense of my life. Illustrated as concentric circles that connect ,What you *LOVE*, What you are *GOOD AT*, What the *WORLD NEEDS*, and What you can be *PAID FOR*.

This tool helped me come up with a clearer idea of my ikigai, a profession that is line with who I am and would like to be. (diagram on pg 32).

While we're at it, since I love etymology, let's look at the word *integrity* for a second. It comes from Latin interitatem, which is described as *soundess, wholeness, and completeness.* You'll see the prefix *inte* in other words like integral, integrated, and intellect, because they are all related to the word *integer*, which is a WHOLE number, not a fraction., Having integrity doesn't mean doing everything right, it means honoring the whole self. For me honoring my whole self is an act of self-care because it affirms my worth as an individual and instills in me a sense of confidence.

The worth or personal value I speak of has nothing to do with my actions, necessarily, but is a product of the investment in me made by parents, family and community. Also, my self-worth comes from my existence as a conscious being. My life, agency, perspective, and attention are forms of capital that hold significant value in the spiritual sense, but in the material world as well. Claiming this value and being discerning about how I put it to use is the most significant part of being self-determinant and autonomous.

I don't think we should think too highly of ourselves, but we do need to feel worthy of love and respect. My sense of worthiness is what justifies my own investment in bettering myself, but it also shows others that I am worthy of their respect and investment as well. Without confidence, the Golden Rule, treat people thow you would like to be treated, really isn't all that golden. If I don't feel deserving of being treated well, the whole social apparatus begins to crumble. Self-esteem and confidence boil down to self-love, and it requires that I know myself well enough to love the person I am (humility) and be willing to express all that I am (integrity) even as I seek to improve it (practice).

I used to think having integrity meant sticking true to who you are without wavering. Meaning if someone asked you to do something that compromised your identity, it was showing integrity to reject that action and hold on to what you believe.

My feelings have changed a bit. I am beginning to think that showing integrity actually has more to do with being willing to completely compromise you are now for who you want to be in the future, or for the world you want to create. To serve the greater good, we've got to have greater goals. My success is defined by long term benefit that extends not only beyond myself today, but into the future as well

I used to say, "I am just not good with spreadsheets, it's just not my thing." But then I took a job as a logistician and was forced to create reports that projected demand based on anticipated behaviors and trends that all had to be put in spreadsheets. I got pretty good at them and before I knew it, one thing that HAD been true about me was no longer true.

Maceo WAS a guy that was not good at spreadsheets, and NOW Maceo is a guy that is pretty good with spreadsheets. And yet my values are the same. So what I thought I was calling integrity was just empty stubbornness—an unwillingness to change my characteristics in the pursuit of living out my values. In this case, acquiring a skill took a lot more stress and strain than it needed to, as I tried my to hold onto my identity as the *No Spreadsheet Maceo* of the past.

What defines us is not a set of physiological characteristics or personality traits, that never change but our choices, actions, and the base, our values and tastes, those too are subject to change.

It seems that even though I do many things contradictory to a version of myself that once existed, somehow I still manage to live with integrity, by allowing myself to move towards fulfilling the values of honesty, service, and creative expression.

Ikigai diagram with my responses.

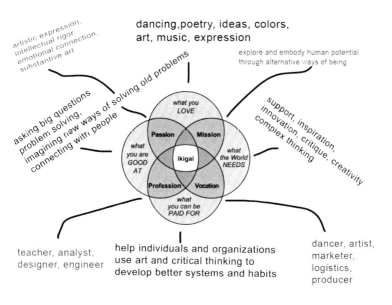

B R E A T H E.

Poem: They've Stolen All The Mirrors
they've stolen all the mirrors.
catch you looking in the river and call you vain.
for wanting to know yourself
for wanting to check yourself.
is my hair out of place?, you ask
and they call you foolish
say there are more important things
than being seen how you want to
—-

they've stolen all the mirrors
reflected back in warped glass, think yourself ugly
not knowing your skin glows
not knowing your own smile
"THIS is what you look like", they say
and you believe them
because how else will you come to know
who you are without them
——

they've stolen all the mirrors
a foiled cellophane will whisper your identity
through crinkled noise,
through hologram.
your eyes can not be described
an abstraction at best
no metaphor can analogize
the experience of you
—-

they've stolen all the mirrors
taken from us all but those with silver plates
who eat very well
who know their place
so you must learn to draw your face from touch
with realism and depth
or else never know
how beautiful you are.

35

B R E A T H E.

SELF-AWARENESS

Reflection. There is a big mirror near the door in my apartment. The purpose of this mirror is to give me one final glance at my appearance before I leave the house. It's not that it would be so mortifying to have a little bit of toothpaste on my mouth when I get to my first meeting, but it's an attempt at making sure I am presenting myself in a way that I think reflects who I am. Socrates said, "Be who you wish to seem." Physically, it is pretty easy to look in the mirror and get some kind of feedback about myself and have feelings about what I see based on the truth in my reflection. Seeing our inner self is so much harder because there are less opportunities to reflect. We are less attuned to interpreting the feedback we get, and often times that feedback is compromised by the bias of the where it comes from. If I feel like I did someone wrong and I ask five people about my actions, I usually end up getting five different answers. Any feedback I get from a person will come with bias, so I have to take it with grain of salt.

(Sidenote: One of the rumored origins of this "grain of salt" phrase was the Roman emperor Pompey taking his medicine with salt to help with the taste. The implication being that these hard truths are medicine but can be more easily received with a dose of skepticism.)

Assuming the feedback is not biased by the sender, the receiver (me) can be biased and not truly be able accept it. Some people cannot sing, and no matter what they are told about their voice being flat or sharp they have no ability to get their voice on pitch— they are tone deaf. I think the same can be true for our ability to self-perceive. We all have blind spots to who we are. The good news is that for most of us it's a matter of practice to get better. At first we might need that grain of salt to tolerate the hard truths, but the more we become accustomed to handling the discomfort that can come with self-reflection, the easier it is to be open to new knowledge about ourselves. I know I am always growing and changing and that means what I once knew about myself may no longer be true, and there are things I once knew, that I have forgotten.

To start, I have to see my shortcomings as impermanent. There was a time when I couldn't talk, read, or write. Now, I have reached a level of fluency that I could have never imagined before I learned to read. My experience in the world, and within language is completely different now and I am a different person because of it. Interestingly enough, the word fluency comes from Latin word *fluere* which means, "to flow". As an action, flowing is much like breath. It is a process that requires two actions for it to be complete. Exhaling alone is not enough, nor is inhaling. Imagine how stifled our lives would be if we had coded inhaling as painful and tried to avoid it as much as possible. We'd only be taking half-breaths, only living up to half of our potential. This seems like the situation we create when we categorize certain experiences as negative, simply because we experience them as unpleasant or discomforting.

Experiencing critique as an attack is a reflex I try to fight against. There are instances when I am legitimately attacked, but when I get earnest feedback, I try to let it land with me before I immediately reject it. Maybe I am masochistic, but there is a sting that comes with this kind of challenge that I rather enjoy, and I seek opportunities to face personal obstacles. **We deprive ourselves of opportunities to grow when we avoid all instances of discomfort.** Being able to face myself is the first step in being able to face a critique from someone else so cultivating self-discpline is and important part of developing confidence.

Practice. Of course, there is a limit to the amount of critique a person can take, even when it is well intentioned. I gauge my wellness by my ability to sense, assess, express, and adjust to shifts in mood. I use emotions to reorient myself in relation to shifts in environment, and make decisions based the relationship between my mood and the conditions I am in. If I am not able to process my emotions fully or cope, anxiety comes as a result of being stuck in one part of the process— that's how I know I am not emotionally healthy.

Emotionl health is essential to learning, but it has some inherent discomfort. We must be able to respond to this discomfort and remain open to the learning experience. If there is trauma, an event that overwhelms my ability to cope, there's no way I can absorb new information because I am closed off. My point is that vulnerability is necessary for learning because it requires there to be trust that the information being received is valid. This can't happen if there is "grain of salt" skepticism.

 In order to learn you have to be open, to heal, you have to be protected enough to be messy. For instance, when you cut your skin, you feel pain(sense), and that causes a reflex that directs your attention to the area of vulnerability. It also prompts you to cover the wound. The areas where we are hurting are the areas where that need the most attention (assess). What happens soon after, is that blood starts flowing freely to flush the wound (express), and this becomes a scab. This hardening is important but it is not permanent, and after the healing process is complete, the scab falls away and normal sensitivity returns. There may be a scar, but we can carry on in a healthy way (adjust). There must be some reason they say genes are "expressed" in a person, as feelings are also "expressed". Genes characterize our capacity to show certain traits is our environment that actually brings those traits to the surface. They are unshakeable elements we carry with us wherever we go, even though they are not always visible. I surmise that this is also true of emotions. We do not say that we "release" our emotions. It would not be accurate to say that sadness is gone when we do not feel sad, only that our sadness has faded. The same is true of joy, frustration, disgust, and affection. Emotions do not go away but appear and reappear from within. It means that these feelings are never gone from us, as our range of emotion is as much a part of our identity as our genes. We carry emotions with us everywhere we go, and they are expressed when stimulated by our engagement.

Just as our genes are activated by shifts in environmental conditions that our body reacts to, our mind responds by stimulating the expression of various emotions. These fluctuations fundamentally alter our intellectual ability, sensory capacity, as well as our individual characteristics. Just as the expression of a gene can make us look different or react differently to the same stimuli, the expression of emotions can make the words we hear take on new meanings.We do have some control over our emotions by keeping them from being fully expressed, but again, this does not rid us of them. It might be sobering to realize that there is some sadness that is ever present, but perhaps it is consoling to know that joy is always with us also.

Every part of this coping process occurs with any emotional harm or affliction against me. I see it as my life practice to do what is required to maintain my ability to sense, assess, express, and adjust my emotions, allowing me to process changes all the way through. When I feel anxious,

I know the process isn't complete. Our skin is where we sense things in the external world, and emotions are how we sense things internally world. After we are hurt, we usually gain our sensitivity back when the scab falls away and we are healed. After a burn or something very serious we might not get our full sensation back. The same is true for me with my emotional state. If my normal amount of sensitivity doesn't return after emotional harm, then I know there's trauma.

Self-Care. Part of being autonomous is the ability to recognize and admit I am wrong without aid. It takes building checks into my process that help reflect my actions back to me, even when I don't have the tools. I remember singing myself little songs, as a child, to remember all the things I needed to take to school with me. These mantras and rituals are not too different from the affirmations I carry with me now. Additionally, the habits I kept as a child are not too different from the commitments I uphold today.

Physically, it's very easy to recognize the routines I perform that keep me healthy. Eating balanced meals, exercise, and hygiene— things like brushing my teeth— to prevent disease, are all things I do to keep my body working. What is harder to notice are the things I do to keep my mind and heart healthy. People talk a lot about these self-care practices, but they range across so many varying activities, that it's hard to know what's healthy or not. I prefer to think of self-care as mental and emotional hygiene.

I brush my teeth regularly to keep them clean, and I dance to clean my spirit. I eat balanced meals to keep my body fueled, and I consume inspiring and thought provoking content to fuel my creativity. Some of these things are routine, others I do on an as needed basis. I might get a massage if I feel a little ache in my body. I also have regular catch ups with family and friends to alleviate the stress of living up to social expectations. In the same way that there are annual practices like visiting the doctor to screen for underlying illness, I spend a few days in Summer or at least once a year with my father just to reconnect with someone who holds deep insights about me.

Finally, I practice responses to specific events that assist me in coping with trauma. For example, if I break my leg the doctor may give me a cast to wear and physical therapy. Emotionally, I might begin to see a psychotherapy or go on a long trip. In either case, I protect the area that is harmed, and at a certain point begin a healing practice. Responding to trauma might begin with a single action, but could also mean adding long term changes to my daily practice over time, to mediate or prevent residual damage. Self-care is the routine, scheduled, event-based, maintenance of our ability to function as close to our full physical, mental, and emotional capacity as possible based on the present conditions.

Some people classify self-care as doing yoga. Others might say it's curling up with a good book and a glass of wine after a hard day. There seem to be all kinds of definitions floating around. With so much variance it can be hard to know the difference between a commitment, habit, or addiction and which ones are self-care or not. I have set up conditions to help me figure it out:

First, the action must provide an immediate benefit. So a surgery or invasive critique might be helpful in the long-term but it wouldn't count it as self-care.

Second, I must be able to initiate the process on my own, meaning it doesn't require a prescription or a specialist.

The third condition is most important to me. Any behavior that is harmful in the long-term cannot be considered self-care. It's not to say that I can't take medicine for example, but if the long-term effects of anything I do are harmful, I can't rely on it enough to incorporate into my life practice.

There's really no concrete answer for this. It's kind of a catch twenty-two. In order to be healthy, I need to do things that help me maintain my health, but in order to know what those things are, I have to be healthy enough to make that determination. It's taken a ton of exploration, and some risks, to find out what works for me, but that exploration has given me enough perspective to make good decisions. I am a pretty decisive person, a large part of that comes from how connected I am to the end result I'd like to see. Knowing my goal or motivation makes it easier to avoid things that I don't think will help me reach it. The clearer you see yourself, the clearer you see everything else.

Lastly, I consider when making life decisions is asking, "How likely is it that this option will actually produce the expected result?" That one is a little bit of a gamble because I can never be too sure about the things I don't have control over, I have to rely on faith. I do my best to make sure my theories are supported by as much fact as possible but in the end, only so much of an idea can be proven theorhretically before some kind of test has to be performed. Funny thing about the word *choice* is that it comes from an old greek word that means to "taste, test, or vote."

There is a reason people say "exercise judgement"; it's because you have to do it a lot to get better at it. I'm not just calculating and designing to build my life practice, I am also sensing and qualifying how I feel in relationship to my intuition and fullest expression of self. Every belief is a gamble— only bet as much of your reality on them as you can afford to lose. And when I lose, I make sure I learn. The "self" part is fueled by knowing what works and what doesn't, the "care" part is making sure I do what works.

Temptation. All the things that move me further away from being a fully expressive, self-determinant, and healthy person are things I would rather avoid out of personal preference. Developing my life practice has led me to appreciate these personal obstacles because I recognize challenges that are actually necessary in helping me grow. Chief among these challenges is temptation. Buddhism might suggest these temptations are the source of our greatest suffering in life. It's not my belief that I should rid my life of them or avoid them as I would prefer, but instead to view them as opportunities for learning and grace.

Essentially, I see temptation in two forms: premeditated and impulsive. The latter form is really easy to spot, it's the candy bars at the check-out stand, uncalculated risks, and other whims that can amount to costly distractions. We could easily chalk these up to my being caught off-guard, curious, or seeking adventure. To counteract impulses, I try to pause. By taking a breath to notice the reflex and investigate its source I create space to ask, "why am I doing this?" Sometimes it is enough to stop me from moving forward. Other times I find that my impulses are actually tied to deeper longings, and they alert me to an area in which I can improve my life practice.

For example, I really love ice cream, but one summer I noticed I was having it every afternoon— it had become a habit. Ice cream is fine but it contains a lot of sugar, which brings with it other consequences. Later I came to realize, I was crashing in the afternoon because I was low on energy. It wasn't just that ice cream was a nice summer ritual, but I was actually hungry for calories and could have found better ways to snack that had less sugar. By choosing another snack or eating a bigger lunch, I stopped eating ice cream on a daily and it became a special Sunday treat, instead. Sometimes physical temptations mask my emotional needs. I could have been indulging ice cream because it created emotional comfort. A healthy body does not have the capacity to lie. In every sensation there is truth. There is no question to the validity of our desires, the work is to inspect and be intentional about how we fulfil them.

Premeditated temptations are a tricky lot to sort out because it's hard for me to know the difference between a healthy desire and an unhealthy desire. They feel exactly the same. There are a lot of ideals that I have picked up from society that are seemingly pleasant, but do not serve me in Truth. These ideals influence my goal setting and I may actually perceive them as something I need to do, but there have been several occasions when I reached these goals and felt no fulfillment of purpose. Our imaginations fuel these desires and can make the outcomes seem unrealistically good. Because the reward is so far out, it's really difficult to know which rainbows are worth chasing. A rule of thumb I follow is: if anything seems like the solution to all my problems, it's definitely not. I find that solutions to a better life always require many different kinds of changes, and when you add up the cost of all those smaller changes, sometimes the vision we covet is no longer worth it.

A goal to get in shape or put on some muscle might require exercise and change in diet, which are good things, but if I presume that changing my appearance alone will change my entire life I could be entirely wrong. A vision to look differently however might be connected to a longing to feel healthier and stronger. This is a much bigger goal that requires holistic change to the way I view my body, my relationship to food, and even how I spend my recreational time. All this work might not be worth it to just look differently, which could be the temptation. To improve my overall health all that effort could be completely worth it. Every positive change has a cost, so a healthy relationship to any commitment includes recognizing and appraising that cost. Paying the cost requires discipline.

Discipline. Often times the word discipline is associated with power and authority so I want to make a distinction. My father used to "discipline" me, and he would say he was trying to teach me "discipline", but I think that was just a euphemism for punishment. I have come to think of discipline simply as facing the hardships inherently associated with the positive things you want in your life. It is not to be confused with obedience, reward, or administering harm which can be felt as punishment.

Self-discipline is what keeps you on the path to what YOU want. Obedience is what keeps you on the path to what others want you to have.
This is the process I consider:
Are you punishing yourself?

1. STOP.
2. WHY!? 2a.Unless of course you are one of those lucky people for which life is not already hard enough, please by all mean continue... or if you are masochistic and find pleasure in punishment, do not let me shame your kink, continue.

Adding pain and stress to your life because you "deserve" it for not being smart enough to make the right decisions or follow through with your commitments, is unnecessary. Pain is already built into the fact that you don't get to have the things you want, and the punishment for not fulfilling your commitments is not reaching your goals! We don't needs to go out of our way to punish ourselves when reality naturally has consequences.The first thing is I try to do is realize the mistake I made, or where I went wrong. If I didn't know better then maybe just learn from it and don't repeat it. If this is not my first rodeo with that particular slight, sometimes I have to admit it's a personal obstacle that is bigger than me, and enlist some outside help.

Whatever it is, putting a system or safeguard in place that keeps me from repeating the mistake is a lot more effective than psychologically (or otherwise) beating myself down with self-destructive thoughts and behaviors. The goal of discipline is to carve a path that leads to developing new habits and growing into a new way of being. **Discipline is not about pain, it is about PRACTICE.**

Anxiety. This all seems like a lot. Eat right, meditate, contemplate and be introspective; all before having to go out into the world and perform. Pressure can certainly build up to do life "right". Just the knowledge of it alone makes me feel inadequate half the time. As I said before, on my best day I am about 80% of the person I would like to be.

Not discounting the days when I am hangry, lack sleep, or have fallen off my routine. Those days, I am lucky if I manage to be 50% of who I'd like, and this just makes me feel worse. Generally, I am an anxious person, which is why the whole idea of flow appeals to me in the first place. Being in flow takes the pressure off me to be the impetus for action. I get to be a vessel, I get to respond, and yet there is still a purpose within that drives me. I am not always in flow, there are times when I need to push against the stream to grow and learn.

There are nights when I can't sleep, and instead I get up and work, I keep working until I am exhausted and when I have completed working, I sleep like a baby. Sometimes the stillness must be earned. This is how I found that 5-6 hours of sleep is plenty for me. After 7.5 hours I start to have back pain and feel groggy in the morning. I know some people who really need nine to twelve hours, and that is what works for them. I know I cannot sleep until I have done what I am called to do in the world for that day. I don't have a bedtime or use an alarm clock. I sleep when I'm tired, and get up when I'm rested.

From the outside I may seem like the person with the most agitated mind and heart. I am bouncing around between different hobbies, professions, and relationships. Just to describe it would be exhausting, but that is what the whole idea of the tao is— the path. On either side is of the path is chaos, but when you find your own way there can be stillness, even while you are in motion. Beneath my seemingly erratic behavior is crystal clear vision and profound stillness.

Anxiety for me is not the enemy, but an indication that I am not focusing on the right area. If I focus my attention on one thing and it seems like I am making progress, but I still have anxiety within me, then I'll try to divert my attention to something else of interest. Still, there is a difference between what is interesting and what is important. I can refocus and accomplish great things, but still not address that anxiousness or longing. Yet again, I try to find what actions, beliefs, and ways of being will bring me that sense of inner peace. I know that I am in flow because I have no problem avoiding distractions. When I am in flow, everything else in my field of vision is blurred, but I have the intellectual alacrity to shift my focus and keep up with the changes in my environment. Finding inner peace isn't always about simply calming my anxiety, because most of the time my anxiety goes away once I figure out what I am actually supposed to be doing with my time.

Discernment. As conscious and animated beings capable of choice and movement, we are always making connections and relating ourselves to the environment we are in. I think of us as travelers in the universe with all kinds of tools that help us navigate life. Culture gives us references for our identity and social roles that we can accept or reject these roles provide context for us to recognize where we are and how we are perceived. Culture and social norms can only take us so far when it comes to shaping our identities and lives. We might have similar physical characteristics, personal histories, or even similar values and experiences as others but that doesn't mean we are the same person. We can't just follow our social norms blindly. At the same time, it also doesn't serve us to pretend like we are entirely unique in our experiences of life, because that isolation can cause pretty severe anxiety as well. How we shape our identities and innact our ability to self-determine is through the practice of discernment.

All the work I do to maintain humility is so that I can stay in touch with my intuition, its the central reference point that helps me make sense of all the context, stimulation, feedback, and criticism I face in the world. Referring all the my options back to my strengths weaknesses and other characters is critical. Humility is the first line of defense for decision making and choice as it helps me make determinations about what is right for or wrong for me specifically. If I think too highly of myself I might take on more than I can handle , but if I am too modest, I will sell myslf short.

When something resonates with me, I am excited, I am inspired, and I am called to move when it doesn't, I can't force it. Ironically, I happened to be black and there is a stereotype that black people like watermelon, (doesn't EVERYBODY like watermelon?) but I also happen to be allergic to melon. There is every social and cultural reason for me to like watermelon except, it just doesn't serve my body. Just like a tuning fork has a pitch that is very reliable at determining what resonates or not my intuition has its own tune and watermelon is not in my key. We live in a world with a lot of noise, so it actually takes practice to remain connected to that voice of intuition. When I lose touch with my inner voice/conscience/inui I get anxious so I try to stay connected to.

Poem: Running With Scissors

Who said this side or that was the wrong one for the tracks,
Whoever said flight was only for birds inspired mice to
be bats. So they do it they own way. Sleep in the day and
play in the night, And see with their ears as if they can
hear light.

Weird rodents with wings using echoes for sight like
Daredevil.
But in the devil's lair we swear they dwell, 'cause they
think different we scared,
If it don't work like ours then it needs repair.
But what if it just … works.
Our rules don't apply to them.

Maceo be Neo, metaphorically Morpheus orbiting your
world, cuz I'm outside of your agenda.
School of thought I ain't attend, took my classes in the
wind with the hallway breeze,
Where I sit for disruption. Always had too many answers
and too many questions.
And they said I didn't know how to ACT, but they never
taught us how to BE, and they still don't.

Only teach us the rules like there's nothing in between
them.
They bleed over each other like connected gates and bor-
ders. We're never nowhere or anywhere, always
somewhere, in a city or a county gotta keep you in a
jurisdiction.
Their laws don't apply to me, they serve the purpose of
classification and organization
But my definition is defiance, of gravity, naturally.

I remain suspended for not believing in your principles,

instead I set the precedent.

Elected by my own faculty, school of thought accredited by experience.

They told me not to run with scissors, and I ask "why?"

"Because the last little boy who ran with scissors, stabbed himself in the gut and died"

And I see the logic, hospital tragedy, lawsuits and all, but from what I got in math, their equation is off.

There's a variable in my veins they aint accounted for.

I am not the last little boy.

More like the first, to successfully sprint through a crowded classroom with two sets of scissors and not impail anyone except the teacher with the point that I proof.

So I got suspended for not following the rules, for escaping crayon from paper and writing on the walls, and not bending myself to fit within laws.

My lyrics don't fit with the bars, my sentence don't fit with the clause, my cause may not fit within y'all's, but I should no less be allowed to strengthen my jaws.

Stop my dreams, dance in my drawers, run with scissors, talk to strangers, do it on the first date, juggle knives play with fire, become fire if I choose to.

Move outside the rules and make up something new so they gotta make up more rules for me to not follow, laws for me to not obey, take class in the hallway and learn my lessons the hard way.

I would rather, stab myself in the gut and die while running with scissors, than sit in class bored, not living my life to the fullest.

Your rules don't apply to me.

#TAOOFMACEO

Instagram · DECEMBER 22, 2016 · Get cozy with who you are and you will be comfortable in even the most prickly of situations.

Facebook · January 19, 2017 ·
You were born knowing how to float and the world taught you how to drown.

Facebook · May 11, 2017 · Your inner-child deserves the best parenting you are capable of providing.

Instagram · October 20, 2017
Don't be so free that you're lost..

Facebook · July 8, 2017 ·
Use what you got, take it as far as you can.

Twitter · July 14, 2017 · Have faith in what you know and stay flexible enough that being wrong won't break you.

Facebook · August 25, 2017 ·
If you are in the position to judge, you are a position to help.

Instagram · November 8, 2017 ·
Don't let who you were yesterday keep you from being who you can be tomorrow.

Twitter · March 13, 2018 ·
The heart has the engine, the brain has the steering wheel.

Twitter · June 26, 2018 · We scramble for power because we forgot we are already powerful.

ASK YOURSELF:

Am I assertive? What is the difference between assertive and aggressive?

Am I more likely to accommodate others, or seek to have them accommodate me?

How much do I let my perception of what others think of me effect my thoughts and actions?

Am I more likely to exaggerate my accomplishments or down play them? What would it be like to change this behavior?

Do I have a good track record for reaching my long term goals?

Am I generally happy with my place in the world?

True or False:
My friends are lucky to know me.

True or False:
I feel comfortable making others uncomfortable to get what I want.

Consider which statment is more true:
I am my own worst enemy.

I am my own greatest ally.

What is the difference between having integrity and being stubborn?

RELATIONSHIPS

Others. Have you ever noticed that people automatically change whenever a camera is pointed at them? No matter if you tell them to act natural, they can't. There is something about being looked at that changes our natural state to something of a performance. Werner Heisenberg was a German physicist who actually has an equation that proves it. Heisenberg's Uncertainty Principle asserts that there is a limit to the degree that any quantum particle can be measured.

This produces what is called the "observer effect" where the very process of measuring something changes it. The idea explains a little bit about why I think people change when you point a camera at them. The same thing happens when any second person comes into a room. People naturally respond to changes in environment. My hunch is that it is almost impossible to "act natural", when you are aware that you are under observation.

Essentially, any time you are around another person, or can sense that you are being looked at, you change from whatever your natural state is, to a performance. This isn't necessarily bad and it doesn't mean people are inauthentic, but for me it means I want to be aware of my performance, to make sure it is an accurate and appropriate representation of who I am inside.

If I am in a room with bare walls, no furniture, and it's completely dark, my reality ends at the tip of my fingers. But the moment the lights are turned on, I touch the wall or another person in the room, it completely changes my reality to include these other elements. My mind can recognize both myself, and myself in relation to everything else. For shorthand, I call it the *I/Else* concept, where my experience of reality is comprised of myself and everything besides myself, including other people, other things, light, space, time, and other factors.

If it is part of me, then it is *I*, If I can distinguish it as outside of myself, then it is *Else*. Just as I have my own structural integrity, so does everything else. The first thing I do, is get to know myself, so I can recognize what is *I*, and then I can use that reference point to better understand everything *Else*. Yes, it means that everything I think I know, is subject to my own bias, but that is okay because the better I know myself the more capable I am of recognizing that bias, and adjust accordingly. These adjustments affect changes in my behavior, so anytime I am responding to the Else, I am in some kind of performance.

Learning more about my performance helps me hold true to my path even while my natural state it is being compromised by the presence of other things. If there is nothing around me, I would just be carrying on without interruption. Sometimes the influence of the Else in the room is helpful based on where I am called to go, and sometimes it isn't.

I am no physicist, but I am a dancer, and while the fields are very different in a lot of ways, it is helpful to think of a single dancer on the floor the same way you would think of a particle. There is even a term for this atomic dance, called Brownian Movement, named after the botanist Robert Brown who is often credited for the discovery of this movement.

Basically, some objects that would naturally be stationary seem to be moving because they are an environment that is full of motion, the same way a dancer would be if they were on a dance floor. The object may or may not have its own movement, but even still, the environment agitates the object and so it is always moving and responding to the changes.

Instead of thinking of a natural state and performance as opposites, we could actually integrate the two ideas and reach for natural performance. Combining the ideas gives us enough space to honor our integrity, while leaving room to adjust for bias. Naturally the way you dance in an empty room is different than the way you would dance in a room with furniture or other dancers. Instead of only having one way to move, my goal is to pretend that the room is empty so that I can express and communicate freely, but still be aware enough of everything else so I don't hurt myself or others.

FRIENDS

Fellowship. I don't like the idea of being "just friends" with anyone. I believe all friendships are romantic. If I could, for a second, take some poetic license, it might allow me illuminate that there has not been one friendship in history that was cold, stoic, or transactional. Arguably, it is passion itself that defines friendship. Love itself— is the irrational force that compels us to put our own best interests second to those of another. Reason has never compelled me to spend a half day helping someone move for no pay. When I do perform these acts, they are "favors"done as a gesture of love, extending good fortune to another person. The accounting on these IOU's is muddy at best. Oftentimes, a home cooked meal between friends, is worth more than food paid for in a restaurant because it is prepared with love. This care and concern is the most valuable asset we have because at the basis of friendship is generosity. Generosity of time, energy and spirit requires emotional investment, fantasy, romance,and hope. Infact, the original root of the word "friend" comes from old Proto-to-Indo-European languages *pri-yont* meaning "loving" with the root *pri* meaning "to love".

So, if by "just friends", we mean passionless, loveless, recreational—no, I don't like the idea of being "just friends". I would go so far as to say that the entire basis for society is the idea of fellowship. The sense of fellowship is where we find the commonality needed to create culture and society. It all starts from friendship! What's more, is that friendship is not rational, it is emotional. I am not simply making an economic wager about my ability to survive with other people, there is actually an element of it that is pleasant and psychologically necessary. When I think of friendship, it means being open to embracing as much of the totality of a person as they are willing to share. It means striking the right balance between support and compassion. Fellowship implies a shared responsibility to maintain the relationship and contribute. I imagine it as looking like a see-saw where as one person goes up, the other goes down and in the center holding thing together is the bond that changes *I* and *Else* to a unified *us* and *we*. In this case, fellowship takes two individuals and forms a third thing, the relationship, that is co-created by both people.

Belonging is the sense and condition of two or more people meeting the needs of one another. The story of Goldilocks and the Three Bears is a perfect example of belonging, one bed was too firm, one bed was too soft, and one bed was just right. If a relationship is able to be both supportive enough to hold me up, and flexible enough that it is not constricting, then I feel that is where I belong. Recognizing "our people" has everything to do with knowing what our own needs and boundaries are. The generosity of time, energy, and spirit that make up friendship is not limitless. So when we think of the love we share between friends, it is as hard for me to accept the idea of being "just friends", as it is for me to accept the idea of "unconditional love", as something possible or practical. It's one thing to admire someone, or feel affection for them, as these feelings can inform my intentions, but intentions alone are not always enough for people to feel supported. I strive to realize the care and concern I have for people, through my performance of specific behaviors that show support and compassion.The feeling of love may be unconditional, but a relationship takes action.

As a child I had caregivers that loved me and took care of me without the expectation that I do anything in return. If I was crying, they would find was to make me feel better. Food? Nap? Play? And they never expected me to say thank you because I couldn't talk yet. It was an entirely lopsided relationship.

As an adult, love is an entirely different arrangement but we use the same word to describe it. When we get older our needs are far more complex, and these needs are often much harder to accommodate, as the adult relationship expectation also includes reciprocity.

The construct of love in our minds needs to be reimagined from the model of our caregiver relationship (unconditional) to our partner relationship (reciprocal). If we do not adjust and redefine what our expectation for love is, we run the risk of holding adult love up to an 'unconditional' standard that is both unfair to the relationship and detrimental to the health of people in it. Adult love, in friendship or otherwise, isn't necessarily about how you want to feel, but rather how much you are interested in, and capable of, contributing to the maintenance of the relationship.

Partnership. When I think of what is required to keep a relationship going, I think of that same atomic dance as before, but now with two individuals. Partner dancing is different than dancing alone, in that it's not just about expression, tapping into the fullness of ourselves and maintaining health, but it is also about making sure that we are supporting the collaboration. The fundamentals of partnership are in every relationship, whether it be friends, business partners, teammates, family, or lovers.

Commitment, trust, communication, and vulnerability are the building blocks at the foundation of any relationship. These also represent areas with some of the hardest challenges to overcome. This is partly because the give and take between the two people is so intangible. If you are not careful you can get hurt, and once the harm is done the relationship can be put in jeopardy. Once you get into the habit of second guessing your partner, it is very difficult to repair the bond. We already have our own issues to figure out, but it is nearly impossible to know what is going on with the other person as well. To make things easier to understand, I think of all relationships as dance partnerships, as all the elements of relationships are found in partner dancing. It's the work of bringing two dance practices together, just as relationships are the work of bringing two life practices together.

Commitment. A relationship is a lot like a conversation, it requires both people to play their part in whatever activity they are doing— dancing, working together, making love— in a way that works for everyone. You must commit to bringing your best self to the pairing to ensure that you are both comfortable meeting each other's needs in the partnership. The first thing that must be agreed upon is that both people actually want to be in partnership and support each other. Personally, I think it is best when everyone is equally dedicated to the success of the partnership, but sometimes there are imbalances. Things can still work out within imbalance, but it might impact the sustainability of the relationship in the long run. In business and in love, it is important to have some clarity about expected outcomes. If one person is in it for the "long haul" and the other person was only considering something short term, their approaches to the partnership may be different. After I get acquainted with someone, if we are going to deepen our relationship it is important to explore the nature of the partnership and what that means for both people. Because I think so highly of friendships, a smaller number of people fall in that group. I have tons of acquaintances, but I have a much smaller number of friends. Framing a relationship can be formal, like on a contract, or informal, through conversation. There has to be a way to confirm everyone is on the same page. Without this clarity we run the risk of causing harm.

Trust. Once that initial commitment is made, I need to be able to rely on the other person to do their part to support and understand me, and I, them. This isn't just about reciprocity, but it is also about familiarity. Trust isn't just earned, its learned. We all have different skills, tastes, fears, and goals that make us different. Therefore, before going too far in a relationship, a general understanding of each other must be established, and because we change, that understanding should change accordingly. I personally don't like small talk, but I do think it is important to have a foundation of some kind in any relationship. Having the same relationship goal is one thing, but it is important to move at a pace comfortable for each party. If we are dance partners, we've got to match our skills and strengths with each other to know what makes a good connection. As trust is developed, we gradually increase our ability to perform together and the relationship becomes stronger. When I say the relationship is made "stronger" I am speaking to increasing the relationship's capacity to support the needs of the all people in it.

Communication. When I'm dancing with someone we have to be in sync, if we're moving too fast for me, it is my responsibility to let the other person know to slow down. If we need to speed up, they communicate that to me as well. If either of us ever feel unsafe, we both have the authority to bring things to a halt and regroup. We check in, physically, by re-adjusting our bodies and keeping eye contact. Without this, my partner may not know that we need to make adjustments in how we engage with one another and I could fail to support them. A misstep on either end could lead to injury.

In friendship, I look for partners who can communicate their boundaries and expectations as well. This is tricky, because in order to be able to communicate our boundaries and goals, we actually need to know what those boundaries and goals are in the first place. For me, ethical behavior in relationships requires some degree of personal inventory. There's always going to be bumps along the way, but even then, communicating when we have been hurt is super important. In any partnership, I like to check-ins and confirm that the information I need to relay is being received and understood, while also making sure I'm receiving their message, so I know where we stand. As dancers we are always listening to each others' bodies to gather information about weight and speed and style as we move together. We can only perform at a level as high as both of us are comfortable going. It takes two to tango.

Vulnerability. Fear is invariably going to come into play, not only for the me, but for my partner as well. We are forced to confront our own insecurities and fears with another person because they are there to witness them as they surface. They can be clear blocks to progress in partnership. In dance, if one partner tenses up and grips the other person too tightly because they are afraid, it can slow things down or cause injury. If we are doing complicated moves, we can easily get hurt by a rogue limb flying around because one or both us are not paying attention. In relationship, the more intimate things become, the more complicated they become. We must be open to the possibility of being hurt, all the while doing everything we can to ensure the other person is taken care of. I acknowledge that I am vulnerable, particularly because I am not omnipotent. The selflessness is, at times, the glue that makes the bond stick—my partner is looking out for me and I, out for them. We are neither fully independent, or co-dependant, but interdependent, sharing agency to accomplish both common and individual goals.

What happens as a result of these connections, is that every so often one of us will receive a thrill of accomplishing something they never could have accomplished alone. I get just as excited to support another person's growth. When everything lines up, both people click and find a harmony that may last an instant, or an hour. It is that harmony that we are really searching for in our relationships.

That zen, meditative moment we arrive at whilst dancing is symbolic of the possibility within all of us to connect to everything else around us. Commitment, trust, communication, and vulnerability are notions we hear about all the time, but in dance they come to life visually and physically. It can also reveal the truth of two people's incompatibility as well. One person may favor expression, while the other person favors connection. It often comes down to priorities. Dance is the physical mirror that reflects our mental and emotional changes.

It's as if the same physical laws of gravity apply: to keep us from falling emotionally, we need to support each other. When you fall in love, there should be someone to catch you. To paraphrase Sir Isaac Newton,
"Objects in [e]motion wish to stay there."

BREATHE.

Poem: Objects In Emotion
Objects in emotion wish to stay there
I am Newton I am Cupid I am Poincare
this is my conjecture on romantic relativity
I am Einstein I am Tesla I am Socrates.

Creativity is sexy intelligence, the new black,
she has algorithms tattooed all along her back.

Her ovaries hold solutions to evolutionary problems,
lingerie in the shape of geometric patterns,
brain mass is massive and all the right matter
and all the right spaces, in all right places.

She's the ultimate equation clear eyed dreamer,
proof to all my theory, spits philosophy through lip gloss,
cosmetic cosmos.

I'm pondering the possibility of metaphysical bliss,
estimating the reaction created if two souls were to kiss.

Subatomic attraction so we can't blame gravity,
she's spice on strings, nice on neutrinos,
to oppose the proposition would put a schism in the galaxy.

And it's not all jargon, chemistry is arsenic
reciprocated 'i like you' s elevate heart palpitations.
Energy transference over distance is magnetic
friction sparks between us, she's sweet. i'm diabetic.

Live lighting created on an alternating current,
we dance at light speed on an asynchronous circuit.

There is science in all art and vice versa,
our experience is more than just the surface.

The past is a bit faster than the present,
so the future can't afford to be hesitant.

Interaction with each other is no way inhibited love is a
primary force non derivative.

The end only leads to the start,
thoughts only guide you to your heart.

Didn't know freedom existed until I risked nonexistence
life can be much more than the pursuit of subsistence.

You'll never see the truth less you lessen your lies' opacity.
You'll never fill your heart if you never test its capacity.

Every person is potential, energy is everywhere,
and objects in emotion wish to stay there.

MORE THAN FRIENDS

Attraction.

Love is such a big topic. It has been talked about and written about so much that my input might just be adding to the noise. I have done a lot of my own thinking on the topic, and the most simple definition of love that I use is: the experience of resonating with the parts of ourselves we find in others.

There are other elements of love beside resonance, like affection, care, and action but this is a great starting place for my understanding. Sometimes it's easier to resonate from similarities because we are in the same family, have shared history, or common or complimentary characteristics. Of course, we all share the common element of humanity, so there is potential for an unconditional, or universal, human love but because that is so common, we often overlook the significance of our similiarities for our differences.

We also connect to people based on attraction to characteristics we admire. Physical attraction could be based on sex, beauty norms, status,or smell. Emotional attraction could be based on comfort or support. Intellectual attraction could be based on stimulation or affirmation, and each one of these categories can me mixed or interchanged and multiplied. I realize I am attracted to many different kinds of people for many different reasons, yet the underlying commonality is some curiosity, or hope, that what I imagine is true about the experience I could have with them, is worth exploring.

Sidenote: I think this is the perfect time to note that there is a big difference between attraction and compatibility: I can be interested in a person because of my own ideas about who they are and be completely wrong, or they can be attracted to me because of how I appear to them. In either case, it takes giving people a shot to find out, and just because there isn't compatibility doesn't mean they, nor I, are any less worthy of love. We just might not be be the best support to each other to create a healthy relationship. Just because we are a match, doesn't mean we are a fit.

This compatibility speaks to all the different areas of connection that we have in relationship. To me, friendship is underneath every strong relationship of any kind. Romantic relationships as we call them, require all the work of platonic friendship and the additional support needed to maintain the romantic elements as well. **Friendship is the cake, romance is the frosting.**

Romance.
One of the first big questions I asked of society was *What is the difference between admiring someone and having a crush on them?*

In general, the answer that I got back was that you can admire your father or mother but a crush is a romantic feeling. As I began to further investigate this idea of romance I found that, aside from a feeling, one of the biggest parts of romance is intimate, physical touching. Kissing, petting, sex— these physical acts and the desire to perform them is what really draws the line between what most people call platonic relationships and romantic ones in an observable way. What is tricky about these gestures for me is that not all of them are clearly sexual, sensual, or affectionate. For some people, hand holding is intimately romantic, and for others it is platonic. In different cultures all over the world I have seen hand holding, kisses on the lips, and close cuddling that was all done in the name of platonicism. Romantic relationships aren't just about the actions either, it's really about how we feel about the actions and how we feel about the other person enacting them, that makes all the difference.

If we take every miscommunication that is possible between two people and pour the additional connection that comes with romance onto it, we radically raise the stakes in terms of our ability to help or harm in a relationship. Romance is very hard to describe because we all experience it so differently. Personally, it is very tied to conversation, intellectual exchange, and visual and physical attraction. Whether sensual or sexual, the way that I recognize romantic love is through my body, whether the expressions of romance are verbal or emotional. Beneath it all, affection, intimacy and authority are the three basic elements that make up romantic love as I experience it.

Affection.
The feeling of "butterflies" in our stomach that people describe when their crush comes around points directly to the root word of *affect*-ion meaning, "to have an effect on, make a difference to, or move emotionally", is what we feel when we see a heart warming film, or when we see a cute baby or puppy. It is an irrational, visceral response, and it isn't always pleasant. This is why the word "crush" has a slightly negative undertone. Affection awakens a longing in us to be close to whatever we are responding to. It is enough to draw me across the room to talk to a beautiful stranger or stand in line for hours for an autograph from someone I really admire. This feeling can be fueled by many things, but its nature tells me that it is something kind of the opposite of the fight or flight response. I call it the *love or linger* response, because I sometimes find myself staring or fumbling over my words, without truly being in control of my actions. Honestly, it makes me feel foolish and I don't like it at all. From this foolish state, I become

unable to establish any successful guard or boundary because what I really want is to decrease the amount of space between myself and the other person, to no space at all. We all want to connect, but with limited time and so many people around us, affection helps me make sense of who I should be connecting to.

Intimacy.
To have deep connection, that is, to share myself, I need to be in touch with myself enough to be open. People have been talking about emotional availability a lot more these days, and I like that terminology because it speaks to the reality of whether a connection is even possible. It's just like booking time in my calendar for a meeting. I might have a strong desire to connect, but if I already have something in that spot, then my time is occupied with something else. My time is limited and so is my emotional capacity. The way we understand our world is so physical that we talk about it in terms of space and distance. Intimacy is really a profound emotional closeness and that requires giving another person access to our emotions. It makes us vulnerable to harm from them, but it also creates the opportunity for transformation. We say that we are "letting someone in", when we are intimate, which speaks to the development of trust in a relationship, but also the creation of a new sense of our own self that includes their input. Through intimacy I begin to include another person in my thought process and decisions as if they are an extension of me. *Me, myself, and, mine* become *us, we, and ours*. Romantic intimacy can fundamentally change our experience of being human from one that is always lonely, to something the feels more complete. We are deeply affected by those that we have intimate relationships with. The people we are close to shape us.

Authority.
Love can be really exciting. It can also be really scary because we recognize its ability to impactful our lives and to transform us.

Love is power(ful).

Love is power, and I mean that seriously. Once we let people into our lives and give them space, we have little control over how their actions affect us. If a random person says they don't like my writing it makes no difference to me. If someone I love says they don't like my writing, it has the potential to really damage my self-confidence in that area. I expect the people who love me to understand me, and I rely on them to remind me of the best parts of myself when I forget. A large part of my self-worth comes from my relationships, so when they fail to support me, it's almost crippling. On the other side, when I am in love with someone who loves me, I feel capable of almost anything. In that way, it is very similar to the love I have felt from my parents. No matter what I did wrong, even when they disciplined me or were upset with me, I always knew they they understood me and held compassion for me. Affirmation and that feeling of understanding are so important to me, it gives whomever I seek that affirmation from a lot of influence over me. I want to stay in good favor with them, and have heavily invested in our relationship so I am more likely to make additional compromises to maintain it. Giving another person this kind of personal authority makes no rational sense, but it's why we hear about people that are "fools in love." Romantic love transcends rationality, and to be in love requires surrender.

Love is powerful. Just as the bonds between atoms are powerful, the bonds between lovers are as well. Love, in all the ways that it appears, is an emotional power that is just like a physical power, that having the ability to transform us. It is the jet fuel that has the capacity to move us towards transcendence into our best selves and having the most valuable experiences during our lifetime. That power can be seen between the teacher and student— where the ignorant becomes the wise, or between the parent and their offspring— where a child becomes an adult. It can also be seen in the experience of awakening new parts of ourselves that we did not realize were there. Like a psychedelic drug, love opens our capacity for all kinds of new experiences, but we must be open to it.

I always try to recognize the moment when I give , or am given, this authority. When you take every kind of mistake or miscommunication possible between two people and add to it this degree of influence and potential for change, it means that we have a responsibility to make good on the trust and vulnerability of ourselves and one another. Having someone laid out on a operating table with a scalpel in your hand, there is significant risk of creating great harm, even though there is the potential we could be of great help. Again, knowing my own capacity to support love in relationship is important so that I don't inadvertently harm myself or others.

Grief.
With all the power that love has to affect us, the absence of love can be very painful. I don't think that every relationship is supposed to last your entire life, at least, that hasn't been my experience. I have had some very profound connections that will have lifelong impacts. I will carry those experiences, and pieces of the people whom I have shared them, with me until I am no longer here.

There is a temporal nature within all things and being willing to accept the seasonality of our interactions is something that I continue to grapple with. Love is a continuous force that is pervasive in my life, but I don't believe that the relationships, in which I experience love have to last forever.

Loss is about the least romantic thing to think about, but if I am going to open myself up to loving someone wholly I want to understand the risks. Whether a relationship ends because the person moves away, the result of a break up, or even as a result of death, all relationships end.

I have dealt with losing love in several ways and what I glean from the experience is that when we are in love with someone, part of our existence is tied to theirs, and when the relationship ends we lose a part of ourselves as well. Therefore, it can disrupt our whole world and sense of identity.

Grief is a reckoning, the process of realizing that what we hoped or believed to be, is not our reality. I tie it to relationships because whenever I engage with others, I am constantly adjusting, coping, and shifting to be in touch with the reality of our interaction. It's not just my story and life experience that get to be true, but that of another person who is just as complex as I am. To be able to hold space for this requires understanding, but it also requires resilience and those are qualities I am always working to cultivate.

The greatest loss I have ever felt was when my mother died. She was my whole world of love and our connection was one of the cornerstones of my identity. It was my mission in life to make her proud and make good on the love and sacrifices she made for me to enjoy life. When she died I realized that I was ill-equipped to handle such a drastic shift in my perception of self and reality. My world was broken in disbelief. The smallest things tore me apart.

From Facebook · December 29, 2017 ·
GRIEF & DISBELIEF:
When you are riding the train to work and a little bird flies by and you burst into uncontrollable tears and you try and stop yourself because you are a grown ass man and it's 5 years later, the people around you are in disbelief.

Your position on the idea that your mother "is always with you" when you never see her or hug her, or laugh at her, when she never subtly mentions that you don't call enough, you are in disbelief.

If grieving is the reconciliation of what you thought would be with what actually happened it is disbelief. It is not being able to wrap your head around the idea of always, or never, or forever.

Grief is pervasive and unexpected, it is so fucking unfair it makes the whole universe seem like a losing hand. If after so long it's only marginally easier to live with the quiet pain, answer phone calls, and let people into your heart, you are in disbelief.

Moms are not supposed to die, ever. Somebody got it wrong upstairs. I'm angry. I'm sad. I'm still trying to figure out what to believe.

———-

The same has been true for every romantic love I have had. I am very quick to attraction, but I move trepidatiously into the waters of love. Because of my nacent fear of the relationships, undoubtedly catastrpohic end, I am not quick to forge these bonds or give up this authority. Additionally, I want to give my partner enough space in my life, to be themselves, without feeling hindered by me.

It takes so much for me to build intimacy, that when the relationship changes, it can be very difficult for me to understand much of anything else in my life for a little while. I recognize that this process of grieving is difficult but is so necessary for me to regain a foothold on my existence, and renew my capacity for love. Grieving hurts, but on the other side of it, is the opportunity for new hopes and beliefs that are rooted in a firmer, fresher, understanding of myself and reality. This is grace derived from wisdom, it is what brings us back. Some might call it salvation. We just have to be strong enough to endure the grief that we will inevitably encounter on our way to salvation.

Lust.
Recognizing that all relationships are temporary, I tend to focus less on duration, than intensity and connection. I think all love is rooted in friendship, but there is no time-frame on how long it takes to build a bond of commitment, trust, communication, and vulnerability, it can take months, or it happen the moment I lock eyes with someone. In so many ways, being in love is like being in flow, it takes more than just the reason and thinking to navigate a relationship, it pulls you towards something beyond our current moment.

In addition to this, there are more surface level feelings that have to do with the body that are no less honest or true. I think of these connections like electricity, you can get a little jolt, that would be enough to spark an engine, or you can spend time making something huge that can light up a city. It just depends on your intention.

There is divine potential in this thing we call lust. It is definitely related to love, but perhaps just not quite as developed. If love is a meal, lust is a snack. Snacks can be good. They tide you over until you have the capacity for something larger. They can also spoil your appetite and support bad habits. I really value short term romances because they are great transitional relationships that can help us regain our emotional footing and practice the kind of skills we will need in longer term relationships. The key is to always communicate our expectations. Some say that one person always ends up "catching feelings" in a non-committed relationship, but I think the duration of the engagement doesn't mean we don't have to commit.

When things are casual, communication should still be open and honest. I like to know what the stakes are, and as

I said before, check in about how much authority a person is handing me in their lives.

The worst thing I can do is find myself in situation where I am manipulating someone because they have strong feelings for me. At the same time, it is important to keep note of what my motivations are. Bad habits can form quickly, and a diet of snacks is simply unsustainable. If the intention is to be light and fun, we need to make sure that we both have that understanding.

Lust, when done right, can be rejuvenating, educational, and therapeutic. At its best, lust is connected to play, giving us the opportunity to explore and try on new selves. A lot of what I have experienced in my dating life began as lust, and grew into something deeper as we got to know each other. Love and lust are not a matter of length of time, but how we spend the time we share.

B R E A T H E.

Poem: Pterodactyl Love Song
We just talking to fill the silence. She's fly, i'm a pilot...

Careening at full throttle with goggles on wings sharp enough to leave a tear in the air at speeds fast enough to dry the tears from her eye

But too spastic to land any place, i nest on clouds, never really grounded.

Beneath her jeans is heaven and i aim to unzip the sky of their blue

i'm in a helicopter that thinks its a hummingbird staring into the windows of towers like flowers.

i'm a cave man on the back of a pterodactyl singing a love song to a canary

We make an unlikely couple but all day over my head i got a bubble with her face in it and replacing it is futile

Cus' it erases what ever is in its space like she belong there She's posted in my brain like an old man on his porch in a lawn chair.

i am lice and she got long hair
so i live in it. we are an odd pair.

Two left feet so we don't dance much.
Hands touch to lock fingers with no keys

i take kisses with no please, she smiles but no cheese,
i'm blown away with no breeze.

She's a masterpiece and i have a hard time finishing things i got a lotta bottles filled with sticks that were supposed to be ships.

i make omelets outta eggs that were supposed to be chicks, i never cash in my chips.

i'm distracted already, bored with courtship.

i wanna press my hands into her flesh in a way that re-shapes her life.

Kiss her like its the first time i ever done it

i'm such a puppy i bark excitement in sentences that don't make sense and she just thinks i'm clever

She just thinks i'm sweet cus' i use beautiful when i talk about her face.

The arch of her eyebrows, blades of grass, the waves in the ocean , and the curve of her ass categorize my favorite views we are in a stage i can't wait to get through.

i'm tryna build a rocket out of words, my heart burns cus this has so little to do with sex it sucks that this is the best our bodies can do to get close.

How trite it's become and abused by others until its watered down

We took the perfect metaphor for the purest connection and make it cheap thrills

The openness of nudity, undressed from secrets, full contact body language we made drunken bar fight, sloppy kung fu, disrespectful to the art. No. Can't call it sex.

i want to have sunrise with you.

Put the world on a skillet and let the yoke bleed out slow.

Two souls scrambled with paprika, oregano, trumpets guitars, a drum solo, and a big ass curtain that lifts up right before the orchestra starts and a mass choir to sing the chorus.

Let's have concert!

i'm tryna find a tuxedo and a baton, i'm waving my arms like an air traffic controller, i'm djing the stars. telling the aliens to land here.

Let's break the land speed barrier on the way to this collision, so fast that it seems slow from far away.

So fast that the sound... comes... 3 seconds later.

i am not a mack, i am a mach 5 pilot and she is fly, the roar is the zipper on her levi's amplified

We have to call it something else cus i don't want to do what they do.

Let's invent a new vent to release or at least lets lace it with love, passion or some blue stuff that goes straight to your brain, 3 letter,s ain't a long enough name.

This is is not a plane,
It's a supersonic pterodactyl
Me, Tarzan you, Jane.

84

Tarzan! Jane! Tarzan! Jane! Tarzan! Tarzan! Jane! Jane!
'Til it sounds like "Tarzane"

Let's not get freaky but instead just creative,
Like if you got naked and I painted you,

But I was naked too and there was no canvas or brush or paint around

What if we sneezed at the same time while we kissed at the hips, i know i am not making any sense

But i am a puppy and i don't bark in english so a lot is lost in translation.

Since the beginning of time we been having sex, but i would like to do something else,

That feels like new wisdom in a fire pit, black magic over ice cream, the hokey pokey in Cirque de Solei.

i wanna hold you, 'til you can't breath no more,
And i can't breath no more.

But we don't need to.
i want to see you,
The way Our Father does,
i want the universe on my tongue.

And it will taste like a pterodactlyl singing a love song to a canary.

♥

Timing.
When it comes to relationships there is no truer statement than, "Timing is everything." I personally don't even believe in time as a concept outside of relationships. As an individual travelling through life I am never late or early, just always present. But when it comes to meeting other people at specific places, time is an agreement we make about when to meet. Relationships are no different.

In my view, time itself is just a measurement of relationships, and relationships, are all based on agreements. What connects all objects in space is time, what connects all people in relationships are agreements. The people I have interest in change, just as I change. With everything subject to movement, we make agreements about what to hold in place to sustain the relationship. When things don't line up, it creates conflict. My sense of time helps me to understand how many relationships I can maintain or have room for. I might want to meet someone for cofee, but lack the availability in my calendar, I might want to be intimate with someone but lack the emotional availability. Each season of my life has its own needs and timing, and even though it can be challenging, I try to remember that everyone needs to go at their own pace.

Journal Entry · September 18, 2015
On Freedom:
engagement rings on instagram never had me effected,
now im in my feelings thinking about my choices
she's found the guy i spent so much time trying to convince her i wasn't,
after spending so much time making her feel like i was,
when her argument has always been that I could be...
...if I chose to.
one of a so few women who has ever been able to slow

me down
and of course i thought her love was a burden
i didn't really know the value of roots
she, too disinterested in flight or too afraid of heights
too interested in her plan...
...or maybe just knew we would need some where to land
it's so hard to let someone change you without resentment
oscillating between wanting "the perfect" and the present
what good are all the choices if none of them are what you need?
what is the difference between infinite curiosity and infinite greed?
and of course i think she can do "better"
but "better" wasn't wise enough at the time
or maybe she is the teacher i always told her she was
and this, her greatest lesson taught in absence.
i comment jokingly that im jealous...
...but im not sure its funny
i question the stance i've taken for so long
how its served me, and who has been hurt by it
so this is for all the lovers i never put first.
is it misogyny or something worse?
that tells boys to make pyramids instead of homes
as if the greatest art was not the arch.
as if being a warrior is worthwhile without a kingdom
as if all of these riches were not to provide for a people a person, or a family
....or maybe
it is that my greatest fear is that this world is too big and bad for me to be a dad
that until i am satisfied with its state i am petrified to procreate?
that it is easier to shift and entire social paradigm
than to look in to a child's eye and say daddy failed.
but what is courage if not movement in the face of fear

and as the last days of my childhood have grown near
I remember my own father
who was once also an artist
who gave up stock options for baby blankets without a
knee jerk claiming my brothers life and mine as his greatest work,who says it is infinitely worth it
And I think about the King's and Kennedy's and even
Steve Jobs and what men sacrifice to be gods
but my grandfather is a titan in my eyes
and i don't know anyone who owns any of his designs
I am not mourning my inner child
but acknowledging that from time to time he will have to
step to the side as tears fall from my face i know that this
pit in me will be filled in the next chapter
...life is not only about the now but about the after.

And all of my magic and grace and sexy and fun and flight
is still mine but now I have something new to add to the
twinkle in my eyes ... I am wise

I have no need to rush towards anything or run
I have everything i need to handle whatever comes
be it, famine, war, success, or heaven help me... love
it is the biggest challenge I have ever endured; to claim a
title I have always wondered if I could wear.
not soldier, not artist, not genius, no ... I am MAN
and my gift for taking on this challenge is not just fantasy,
but Freedom.

———

Family.
It's crazy to me that generations of bloodlines have been
started by first dates and chance encounters, but truthful-
ly a family starts with two people. I am alive only because
my mother and father fell in love. I have cousins only be-

cause my grandparents had kids, and their kids had kids. The love that is shared between the people in my family is an extension of the love that was felt between the people who started our family. My sense of identity, my name— all come from this connection. As a member of this group. I feel some degree of debt to the legacy of my parents, grandparents, and other ancestors, to continue that legacy in a way that brings pride to our name and heritage. As an extension of my family, I am a member of ethnic groups, and have a national affiliation that both contribute to who I am, I feel indebted to them. Further still, I am a part of cultural communities, professional communities, friend groups and a society that also contribute to my identity which I feel a responsibility to.

Usually this is posed as a dichotomy between the individual's responsibility to the group, and the group's responsibility to the individual. Instead of a dichotomy I think about a paradigm of responsibility, and a spectrum of care and that we exist within. On one side, we have an responsibility to keep ourselves healthy, but that is impossible without a healthy environment. On the other side is our responsibility to contribute to the maintenance of our environment for others which, inherently benefits us as well.

Family is a community affiliation by biological or legal relation. This affiliation makes the bonds very strong and the commitments very serious. My own life connects me to the other members of my family, and the lives of other people I love, and by extension everyone else. This social network creates the mesh we all contribute to and take from, so that no one falls too far below or behind.

The challenge with family is that it's sometimes hard to reconcile the actions of others I am close to with the actions that I would take personally. I find myself in compromising positions trying to honor both the legacy I am a part of and my personal well-being. So the question always comes to me: *What's blood got to do with it?* For better or worse, biological similarity is unchangeable, and for a bond some people will go to the ends of the Earth while for others it means very little.

I want to pay back these social debts to family, culture and society, for how they have supported my in becoming who I am but I don't want to feel exploited. On the basis of acceptance and investment, I can accept the choices of any of my family members as their own without judgement. I can love them, in spite of the harm they do to others, themselves, or me, but that does not mean I am obligated to continually invest in communities of any kind that are not healthy. I think of the paradigm of responsibility as a question about which groups I feel most connected to, and prioritize my contributions alongside those connections. I am an American, but before that, I am my father's son, even before that I am my brother's brother. If my country should ask me to betray my family, the answer would be "No." Although blood is important, our connection is not solely based on blood, it is based on my connection to the individuals or the group affected by my decision. Blood relationship is a consideration, but it is not always a determinant, we also juggle other idenity affiliations as well.

Unlike most other relationships that come by choice, family is different in that you are born into a family without the choice of selection, but choose to maintain the relationship. Everyone that is family is not a friend. A community of choice requires a practice all its own because it is a system of relationships that are all interconnected.
Getting the balance right takes work.

Journal Entry · September 20, 2016 ·
CATEGORIES:
It is hard as f*ck to know who you are! We have so much external stimuli that makes it difficult to tap into our intuition and purpose.

Society has guard rails in place that help us know where we fall based on the family we were brought into and the places we have lived. There is great values in this.
Sometimes though, these guard rails act as gates, that constrict us from exploring other options for how we might live. These gates keep us from understanding members who live outside of the groups we were born into and learning more about other ways of life.

When we don't have the opportunity to learn, we lean more heavily on the established beliefs we inherited. As we age, it becomes harder to let go of the established ideas. This doesn't mean we don't have options, they may just be harder to see.

We can not force people to let go of the ideas they have inherited. In many instances these ideas are fundamentally attached to how they see themselves. And again, it's hard as f*ck to know who you are! So it is understandable that people have ideas about the world that are not true in the objective sense, because our experience of the world is subjective.

What is frustrating to me is when those ideas manifest as harm to others, not in a position to be protected by institutions that hold ideas with a narrow scope of value.

From where I sit, institutional shift only comes from cultural shift, and cultural shift comes only from shifting how we treat each other, shifting how we treat each other comes from shifting our views about who we are.

As terrifying as it is, we must be willing to explore outside the gates of our family, community, and nation to find out who we are and bring that discovery back into our intimate communities.

The more we do this the more we inspire people to attempt it. It's slow because it takes individual effort and that isn't always something everyone has access to. It is a privilege to be able to see the world as it is and it is one afforded only to those that can see themselves for who they are. Until then, we must be resilient for those who have yet to take the leap.

Foes.
I don't have enemies but I do have opponents and navigating those relationships is as complicated as any other. I try to grant the assumption of benevolence, to whomever I come across. Even though it can sometimes be frustrating dealing with people, especially when I am hungry or tired, it helps me to understand, that everyone is human, not perfect. I am just as likely to be the one causing the harm as anyone else. It's human to act out of emotion, to lose your patience and be reactive, to want to fight for your beliefs, even when they are wrong. It's natural to want to hold on to the reality that you know for the sake of your understanding of the world and your place in it. I believe it is a rare triumph of character to be able to recognize when you're wrong on your own. We already live in a world with so much confusion and misinformation thrust at us that many people cling to the feeling of security their perspective offers, simply for the hope to carry on. I can't be mad at that, because I am no different.

Friends and family help me to stay on my path of our shared values and remind me who I want to be. They support and bring out the best in me. At the same time, some relationships challenge me to live up to who I say I am, despite lacking the support to do so. I try to keep a mix of different people who help keep my vision well rounded and minimize the likelihood that I will fall victim to one of my own blind spots. I think in that way my rivals, critics, and haters are some of the most valuable relationships I have because through their distance and ambivalence, they show me what my ideas and views might look like from someone who doesn't knowing me well enough to give me credit for my intentions. Their feedback allows me to polish my practices of communication and action so that they becomes more clear. I may not care for the judgements they make, but if I their words sting, I know they are connecting to an area of sensitivity, and that exposes areas where I have room to grow.Some relationships are pleasant and sometimes they are unpleasant but each is a learning opportunity and part of a complete life, so I wouldn't change it if I could. When conflicts are nor productive, healthy or cannot be managed, I treat it like I would on the dance floor: create as much space as possible between myself and the other party, remain cordial, and limit our interactions to only whats necessarily.

Apologies.
When things go wrong the only way out is through. We can't make people that slight us disappear from our lives entirely and the impact they have on us can definitely linger. Some say you can't change the past, but I actually tend to disagree. My personal history is all about narrative. Even though I can't change the events that occurred, I have a lot of control over the way I perceive them.

Sometimes people use the word "hate" to describe their feelings towards other people. I've heard before that the opposite of love is not hate, but indifference. In order for someone to hurt you emotionally they have to be close enough to do so. If a person's actions are insignificant to you, they may not occur to you at all. Hate comes from hurt, it is that betrayal, distrust, disappointment, and broken faith that inspires it. What I see in hate is anger and hurt so the only way I could hate someone is if they mishandled the love we've shared, neglected, or maliciously harmed me. It takes energy to hate someone. There is something that marks you and leaves you raw when you carry it. The mark only goes away when the hate is released, so that the hurt can go away and the healing can begin.

Apologies can help close our emotional wounds, giving us the chance to begin the healing process. Forgiveness and apologies are not synonymous. I can receive and accept an apology and still not forgive a person until years later. I become able to forgive as part of my grieving and healing process. When I am fully adjusted to the new reality of my relationship to the world, I am able to once again open up, realizing that one instance of broken trust doesn't mean that everyone is untrustworthy. When there is no apology I have to make sense of my reality without of the other person acknowledging their role in my life and the impact of their actions. That makes it harder, but it is possible. **Apologies are something people give to help themselves move on from the *harm they've done*. Forgiveness is something people offer, when they are ready to move on from the *harm they've endured*.** Both can be restorative in their own right.

Facebook · January 13, 2017 ·
Treat people like you need something from them, like
your well-being depends on them... because you do, and
it does.

Instagram · December 27, 2017 · The thread holding
society together is the assumption that given optimal
conditions, people are good.

Facebook · March 14,2018 · The same rain that ruined
your picnic, ended someone else's drought.

Twitter · June 18, 2018 · I aim not to speak negatively
about anyone, but be very intentional about the compli-
ments I don't give.

ASK YOURSELF:

In times of crisis/hardship, do I seek companionship or solitude?

*Do I hold my romantic partnerships to the same standards as
my non-romantic friendships?*

*Do I have a clear vision/definition of "love" that I can reference
and comunicate to others?*

*Am I a good judge of character? Do I read social situations
well?*

*Do I generally feel accepted and understood in close relation-
ships?*

Am I quick to forgive? Am I quick to apologize?

WORK

PASSION

Change.
When we talk about 'work' most people think about a career or vocation. I like to start the conversation with thinking about work in the physics sense, as the energy required to create change.

If something is one way and I want it to be a different way, work is the intermediary between reality and the ideal. When it comes to my life there are things that I have to do to survive like chores and hygiene, that can also be talked about in this arena but I classify them under broader term *labor*. There are jobs, which is also labor, that I do for others in exchange for pay, and of course other kinds of unpaid labor I do for others that I think of as service. Work, is a class of activities that I engage in to get me to where I want to be, moving me along in my journey, I am working to shape myself and my environment into my ideal.

Self-work is great but, we don't live in vacuums. All the systems, objects, and people in the world that make up the *Else*, all have their own force, like gravity. Everything is connected. I use my force and understand that I am a carrier of energy and am capable of impacting my environment through work. I think it's important that I put some intention into what those effects are.

I am work to become the person I want to be (livelihood), I am also integrating information and responding to changes in my environment (collaboration), while also trying to contribute to the lives of others along the way (service). All these forms of work are how I engage with reality to make various kinds of changes, sometimes to keep things moving, or to stop them, and other times, to bring new things into existence.

Livelihood.
The first of these areas in work is both physical and spiritual/emotional. The work I do that makes me feel really good or that is part of a hobby or healing practice, is a part of my livelihood. No one has to tell me to play music or make art, or work on a puzzle, they are self incentivised activities where the reward is built in and makes me feel more myself. These are often seen as hobbies and sometimes trivialized, but I really believe that self-incentivised activities are one of the biggest parts of Life.

Whatever we get super excited to learn about, or what we could spend all day and night doing falls into the category of "livelihood", because they speak to our natural interests. The word *interesting* comes from old english and essentially means 'something worth investing in'. Much of this early definition resonates with me, because the interests and activities I am called to and organically curious about, appear as opportunities to fulfill something in me. I can take great pride from accomplishing tasks that mean little to anyone else. You see this in sports and art, where the significance of winning particular prizes is fueled only by our desire to do well, not so much the objective importance of the activity itself.

Hobbies are a critical area to hold space for in my life because so much of my experience at a job, and elsewhere in the world, is relatively high stakes. If I don't perform to the standard set by whomever is holding the money, I don't get paid. But when I am doing something I really enjoy, like karaoke, I don't have to be any good at it to get the value from the proces, even though I can still put a great deal of effort, into delivering a great performance. This is the fundamental difference between a job, and a crucial part of my livelihood: Play. If all of life was split into two categories they would be work and play, and it takes both of them to make a living. Play affords me the space to feel and connect with who I am when I allow my imagination to roam, and my inhibitions to fall away. It is a place for free learning, exploration and experimentation. Play is a key aspect of emotional wellness and I believe that it is as important to us as food. Too long without Play, I begin to fall into routines that are not valuable, and I lose touch with my intuition. This feeling is shared by artists, musicians, athletes, gamers, fisherman, yogis, and hobbyists of every sort. When indulging in the spirit of Play we can be transported back to a childlike state of pure joy and reconnect to a sense of freedom that isn't often afforded in the world. Deeply connected to Play is Creativity, youre never wrong in the studio.

I talk about creativity a lot. Creation is the work of materializing ideals and it's damn near magic. It's the closest humans can get every day to directly affect change upon objects, ourselves, and the world at large. If you have felt disempowered it can be something as little as re-organizing your room to remind you that you have a force within you that is capable of making things different than they are. Creative activity is a reminder that our liberty and agency is as inalienable and divine. **To create, is the greatest act of freedom.** It is because of our imagination, that I call it divine. Productivity makes it practical. Imagination + productivity = creativity. Reality is something that is directly experienced by our senses and our mind, but our imagination speaks to what may never be real. It shows us worlds and images that fall outside of the realm of possibility, this is special to the extent that it is one of the only places that we have absolute control over everything that happens. If there is an omnipotent, omnipresent God, governing all of the universe, then we are most certainly a part of their imagination. This is why art, music, and books are so important to us, and to me. They give me an escape to places that are more free, safe, and open, where I can transcend hunger, and pain, and fear and express an uncompromising vision for myself and the world. In this place, in my imagination, I find all of my noble truths. It is even a place where I can do things that are socially unacceptable, without fear of judgement and criticism for living my life. The imagination is anything we want it to be. I think it is critical that we maintain a connection to this space from childhood, especially as we move deeper into the influence from the world.

Understanding our imagination helps us understand our ethics and ideals. It helps us understand what feels right to us and how we'd like our world to be. Our fantasies can be a place with no consequences, and yet reality is full of them. Part of this journey is understanding how much of my imagination I can afford to bring into my reality. This process is the creative work done specifically to change our environment. Amy Whitaker, a friend says that, "A work of art is something new in the world, that changes the world, to allow itself to exist." I follow this and believe that everyone is creative, and that the art we make isn't always outside of ourselves, but often times it is expressesed as how we live our lives. **Don't DO Art, BE ART.**

There is a personal reflection inherent in art making in which the product also implicates us when we view the work of others. Socially, the artist interprets the world through their medium and this grants us perspective that we might not otherwise have access to, but it is still not all that they are. When I push myself... and I mean TRULY push myself out of my comfort zone, my capacity for personal growth and change feel infinite. When I give myself the chance to really imagine what I can be, and not fear what comes up, I access the potential to completely flip my life around. One day I began to move out of the safe and cozy world of art into the treacherous cold world of economics to challenge held views about myself. I went from being someone who couldn't pass Algebra to save their, life to someone who is diving into radical mathematics theory just for fun. When I first tried to solve the Rubik's cube, it took me 3 months but, eventually I could do it in under 3 minutes. One year I read 100 books in 100 days. I don't think I am the same person I was then. I am not sure I have FULL authority over the person I am to become, but I am going to make sure to insert my input along the way.

Contrary to popular belief, fulfillment has little to do with success. I was never a fan of participation trophies in sports, because everyone is not starting from the same place in every endeavor. One person's success story may mean taking their team to the finals, another person's success is just having the courage to try out. I am no different. I set goals for myself that are reflective of what next steps look like for me, and try not to base them on the path other people are walking. I can't let what used to define success for me always be enough. I am also always growing in different ways and I try to find avenues that further that growth, which sometimes means letting go of old ways. I'm leaving a lot behind, some of which I really want to carry. But I'm trying to go places I've ever been, so that means I have to pack light.

It's really a struggle to not let your environment define you. It means leaping deep into the unknown and, in a sad way, leaving parts of you behind. But what you gain is a chance to escape conditions that may seem limiting and land in a space where you have more agency to fulfill your potential. I'm pretty ambitious, but it hasn't always manifested itself in a conventional way. I am not driven to conquer, or compete, I am not looking to compare myself to others but I am fascinated by the idea of a "personal best".

Potential has always been a word that has haunted me: The idea that I have unlimited potential seems like a great blessing and burden. I am ambitious in that I am always curious as to the true nature of my potential. If I can learn a skill I never thought I could have, maybe I can master it, and maybe I can master a host of skills. People talk about the 10,000 hours rule it takes to master a skill, and I have always thought, some of the time it takes to get good at one thing can be transferred to getting good at other things. If you are good at running, you are already halfway to being good at a host of other sports, because running is a primary skill.

Leaning into my passions gives me the space to better myself. Mastering skills is only a vehicle through which I build character and actualize the nascent potential within me. Following the metaphor of work in physics, I am able to transfer potential energy into kinectic energy by putting by ideas to the test through skill development every skill I practice, contrubutes to my learning and development.

BREATHE.

Poem: How I Learned Everything

I learned how to drive stick from playing the drums, I learned to tap dance from playing soccer. I learned to play drums from playing the piano. I learned to play soccer from karate. I learned karate from dance. I learned piano from clarinet. I learned clarinet from the walls of my parents first apartment I learned to dance from my little brother.

There are such things as primary skills and brains fill blanks in images to help you get the picture. Puzzles poems, paintings,pieces,patterns. Patterns are key, and keys close loops to continue patterns to repeat. History, we are keys to. To history. Because if the loop is long enough it looks like a line. Especially from the middle. But that is only a matter of perspective blind, blinds, shutters, curtains, curtains, death, dark, vision, blind. Blind. See?

I think thoughts, the world is just a series of ink blots rorschach tests with no answers, rhetorical questions, hypothetical conversations. Imaginary friends, artificial flavors, and edible phrases.

I cook the same way I write poems, I sketch the same way I compete, I write the way I pack a suitcase. I compete the same way I perform. I pack a suitcase like walking to school, perform like casting a fish on a wish and a prayer and I assume flying is done the same way.

These primary skills are divinely guided. There are no experts because the technique is inherent apparent like DNA instructions for how we look. Trust half of what you see and none of what you hear but actions speak louder than words so that is still only 3/4s of a person. The 22 percent of our brains we use leaves us with 3 percent unaccounted and only 3/5s of me is counted. Must be the faith of a mustard seed we use to move mountains.

No one ever changed the world without being called crazy first.

Cuz what are the odds. The odds are the questions and the evens are the answers. Unbalanced tilted by remainders indivisible to a line only to a pattern where even is level ie. Straight, balanced, and solved. Like zero which resembles the egg that came first and the next is the chicken because you can't count them before they hatch.

Which brings us to one. Oddly enough they don't even teach us what zero does until 8th or 9th grade so we aren't starting from the beginning in kindergarten. More like the middle and don't learn about the beginning until middle school. At any rate we can't count from zero to infinity and both are closed loops, just one is twisted. Like our planet is tilted so unbalanced and moving.

I imagine our planet is an atom. I imagine I am a lion. I imagine a lion is a scale. I imagine a lion is an explosion. I imagine a scale is a song when played in intervals. I imagine an explosion is a mustard seen when filled with faith. Songs on clarinet, hope on a casting rod. God in the water shaped like a fish, the universe an instrument and it sounds like a kid trying to find balance in an ever moving world, odd man out. Painter, packer, poet, piece of history, made of make believe. Fluent in doing with these primary skills.

You see, the best metaphors describe things that are exactly the same that we have come to see as different. Like twins separated at birth, or continents, or lips on lovers. Fit perfectly like numbers in sequence code. The perfect program isn't a program but a system in and of itself with no host. A virus with no host. A party with no host that could go on for days, I could go on for days repeating myself in a loop until I set a record, and that record is history on repeat in a pattern that resembles me. Answering the question of how I learned to drive stick.

I learned to drive stick from playing the drums...

———————

PRODUCTIVITY

Collaboration.
Every member of society has the potential to be a co-architect of the world we inhabit. Artists specifically, play a crucial role in helping us expand what we think is possible. By tapping into our imaginations we can pull down ideas that might otherwise be overlooked due to the glaring realities that are in front of us. I am talking about "us" now because the world is too big for to manage or navigate alone. We need each other, we really do.

The way we empower ourselves to do what we could not do alone is by working together and sharing our agency. Everybody has agency, it is that force I mentioned before— the faculties that we can influence directly through our our own will. Not everyone has power, though, that is a faculty that you can influence indirectly through a vehicle that amplifies our will. Power usually comes through some kind of leverage. We gain this leverage through systems (rules), objects (tools and weapons), and relationships (labor) but beneath power is always agency and will.

It's important to me that I always remember that I have agency, because it helps me to remember that I have choice, and that my actions have the potential to be impactful. A simple way that I remind myself of my agency is breathing. If I can control my breath, then I know that I have agency because my breath is a faculty that I can influence directly through my will. This is the same for me with dancing. It is why I love dancing so much, it connects me to both my imagination and sense of agency.

Knowing that I have agency and others do to, we can share this ability to influence our environment and make greater changes to the reality we are in. It could be a physical change like building a structure, or a social change like establishing rules around what is a good way to live. We see and feel these realities in society because of the ways they affect our behavior. A red light isn't a brick wall, but it will bring you to a stop, because we are participating in a social agreement. And again, these agreements are based on relationships and commitments we have with other people. In some cases these unwritten agreements can be so powerful they affect the way we think, and our private imaginations.

The co-creation of society is based on my input, support, tolerance, or contribution of the ideas that make up our social reality. Because we don't all agree on what our reality should be, what defines our society is always in contest, and it can only be settled by each of us consenting to whatever agreement is on the table. Unanimous agreement in a large social group seems impossible to me so the basis of collaboration, is compromise. In order to work with people we have to be able to give a little, to get a little, and hopefully, we get a lot.

Friendship + Work = Collaboration, the process where we take everything that is a part of friendship and direct it towards a specific action. It requires the same amount of trust, commitment, communication, and vulnerability as any relationship with the added demand of trying to accomplish a task or set of tasks.

Collaboration can take on a many shapes in business and in sports, but still it requires that both parties be in touch with their agency and be willing to bring forth that contribution to support the goal that everyone is laboring for. When I work with people I always try to remember that, if they were the same as me, we'd have the same blind spots and overlap in our strengths. There is a harmony that can be reached, but there is also the potential for conflict during the trial and error process of finding the right collaborative partnerships. When we manage to overcome our conflict our capacity to collaborate expands, but it requires that everyone take on a social responsibility to maintain society, that responsibility is a job. My job is to be an artist.

Jobs.

I am not enlightened. So much of my self-worth is wrapped up in my profession that I don't even know who I am without the work that I do. I compromise my relationships, my quality time, and my personal practice of self-care, all to have a shot at being better at my job. And I don't regret it. I am an artist and I am dedicated to creating and exploring my ideas about humanity. I feel more myself when I am researching and creating than I do when I am doing anything else, and that work is self-fulfilling.

The problem however, is that the world doesn't necessarily value my work and labor at the same level that I do. So when it's time for me to pay rent or charge someone for the work that I do or the contributions I make to society, there is this conflict between what I think I am worth, and what people are willing to pay me. Even after I have built the confidence to ask for what I think I am worth, it is within a world that always seems to want the lowest price for the most value. Along the journey of becoming a professional artist and entrepreneur I have had to reconcile, and continue to reconcile, my own personal insecurities around speaking up for my value. This has cost me money and caused me heartache. I believe that my work is of immense value, not only to myself, but to others, because I have decided to take on artmaking as a profession. When I take on an activity as a profession the focus shifts from doing what is solely fulfilling to myself, to accepting and accommodating the interests of others.

The burden to do things for pay is one that is unique to humanity and is based on a social agreement. Yet, it is truly about being of service while doing what is true in my heart to do. A squirrel doesn't need a job, it doesn't need to do anything besides be a great squirrel to sustain itself. In doing so, the acorns get planted in the ground and trees grow and the squirrel's entire ecosystem is supported by them only doing what comes naturally to them. Therefore, I don't think I should have to go out of my way to contribute to my environment if my job is purposeful. If we could all find purposeful work, then we might find that each of the paths that we are walking might carve space for others to do the same.

Our social contract comes with many things that are counter-intuitive and jobs are indeed one of them. Sometimes I find myself in a situation where I am not being supported with what I need to continue in my livelihood, to grow as a person, and to have compassion love, and generosity in my relationships. When this happens and there is no discernable reason for why I am not being supported, it can cause me to have a great sense of distrust in my environment and also cause me to doubt myself. When the phone is ringing, my ideas are flowing, and I am being paid what I have asked for, I have the confidence of a superhero. When the phone stops ringing, or when people try to undercut my worth as if they don't know my value, I begin to feel like something is off, not only with me, but that there is something unjust in society. I remember feeling at times like no one cared about the things that I do. Thus, in the process of sharing what I do, I can get caught up in trying to bring more attention to my work, even though attention isn't what the work is about. Attention is an indicator of potential impact to some degree, and I do think my ideas have the capacity to be impactful.

When it feels like I am being ignored or that the very thing that is missing from the conversation is the thing that I am screaming at the top of my lungs I might feel helpless, frustrated, and hurt.The key for me here is to respond to the pain, and not become distracted by the desire to avoid this pain, but to remain focused on the value I am seeking to create with my work.

The Paradox of Pay
Since I founded Nous Tous Gallery, I have met so many artists with different ideas about whether or not artists should be paid. You might think it would be an unequivocal "Yes" because everyone loves money right? Some artists certainly feel that their work is valuable in a specific economic context, they wish to be paid for their work. Their intention is to make a living producing art that is valuable to other people and trade it for the resources to buy a house or food etc.

I've also found that some artists consider art making a payment in itself. It is a true labor of love that nourishes them as a personal exercise of mind and spirit kind of like working out at the gym. These artists aren't interested in making a wage for their time. In most cases, their livelihood is tied to a commercial practice or another job altogether and they are willing to invest their time and money into their art without expectation of financial return. These are two very very different perspectives. These aren't the only two, but I believe they represent the essence of what is meant by "professional", the intention to earn pay from a particular kind of work.

When it comes to the work of "community building", I find myself stuck somewhere in the middle. On some level, it requires so much of my time and resource commitment to keep things going, but I also would be lying if I said I didn't personally benefit from managing the space and being a "gallery owner". It makes me think of a farmer who is growing a fruit tree. At first, the tree is just a seed, it requires a ton of water and effort to keep it alive and allow it to mature. Years later the tree produces its first fruit, and it is just barely enough to feed the farmer. After another year, the tree is big enough that it is producing more fruit than the farmer can eat alone.. The farmer then has choices: they can take the fruit to market, they can give the fruit away, or they can let it go to waste. I am not one to let resource go to waste—that, is not an option for me. But when I think to answer "should I be paid" to foster community for myself and others, I have historically failed to find the answer.

To me, it seems like accepting money for this kind of work can potentially create expectations that I am not prepared or willing to live up to. People might think of me as "the help" instead of as "helpful". My goal is to be of service, but not to be a servant. I imagine part of it is communicating my expectations and boundaries to start. Right or wrong, my hope is that whatever value I am providing to society can be affirmed and reciprocated and I think this is what makes pay important at its core. Money as a social tool that helps us exchange value, but does little to help us understand what we value. I am coming to realize that for me at least, payment is critically necessary, but not just because of what I can buy with it.

My work is so deeply personal that there really isn't an amount that would adequately compensate me to do it for some else and yet, I continue because I derive value from the activity itself. This, however, means little to me if the work I am doing is worthless to others. So in the context of society, the gesture of a financial donation carries both symbolic and practical value. When people toss their loose change in the box at the gallery, or when the monthly donations come through electronically, it doesn't just ease the cost of keeping our doors open, but it soothes my soul because I know that people could be doing anything else with that financial resource besides investing in my work. I see this in the economies of community and the various ways we exchange value as people. We show up, we contribute, we listen, and sometimes, when we have it to spare, we invest financially in causes and people we believe in. I don't think that artists are in disagreement about whether they should be paid— it is just that passionate people doing work that imbues their life with meaning understand that there are many ways to receive this payment. With Citizens Of Culture, I am trying to avail dynamic modes of value exchange not only to disrupt the way we think about money but to take full advantage of all the ways people are capable of providing for each other.

———-

Money.
In theory, I think money was intended to be an instrument that allows the fluid exchange of value, simplifying transactions from an inconsistent barter system. One of the major problems is that it works too well. You can point to any object and determine a monetary value for it based on the economic conditions around it.

What is particularly problematic is when we look in the mirror and try to determine a monetary value of what we see. We are not objects, but our bodies are objectified and commodified based on social class, health, age, what skills we have, and other factors. This objectification dismisses much of our personhood to be an actual measurement of a person's value.

The first way to resist this commodification of the body is to ensure our own view of self-worth is not entangled with our economic status. The depth of our social connections, skills, knowledge, imagination, and perspective are all components of what make us valuable beyond the product/service oriented, economic environment. Right after the shift is made, money is positioned in our mind as it was intentionally intended to be— a tool for objective value exchange.

It changes the wealth proposition from accrual of property and means to protect said property, to the capacity to experience humanity (i.e. Health, clarity of thought, and relationships). These non-financial forms of wealth often times slip into secondary status because of the more dominant and immediate pressures of everyday life. It's just that we need to make sure that is a temporary and conditional reprioritization and not a surrender our entire value set to monetary priority.

Undergoing this detachment is no small task given the social climate we live in. It is important to build reminders around us to help reframe our value narrative to support a more holistic view. A sustained effort in this could create a strong enough social fabric to influence the practical structures we see in society via policy in government and business because the demand and desire would be self-evident. While it may be true that "everybody has a price" we have to recognize that when we allow ourselves to be reduced to a flat economic appraisal, we surrender everything else amazing about us that can't be quantified. This is the resistance that we are charged with.

PURPOSE

Activism.

Ever feel like you're being forced to compromise your values in order to make a living? One side of me says that I should never compromise. The other side tells me to be realistic and that sometimes you have to do things you don't like in order to survive. The reality is both. We have to be honest about what we gain when we go against our virtues and be willing to acknowledge our current reality, even while we push against it. You gotta crawl before you walk and it is important to remember patience and forgiveness for ourselves on the days we fail to live up to our ideals. At the same time, never forget the struggles of others and the responsibility that comes with our position. The duality of this causes me anxiety. We must commit to confronting our own self daily. Being "woke" takes work.

To make a better world, we have to become better people, and we need to understand what we mean by "better". Do we mean faster, smarter and more productive? Or do we mean more open, caring, and encouraged to honor what is True for our identities? All the social systems that we have set in place are a product of human craftsmanship. As an artist, I work to clarify my own values which inform my designs influence my behaviors through life-practice, and contribute to shaping my reality. Art specifically helps to shape our reality when it comes to objects, movement, ideas, music, food, and many other mediums. We build cultural elements that express and shape how we see ourselves.

Alongside this, activism is a practice that takes on the function of changing our social world as it pertains to economics, policy, healthcare, education, labor and so much more. Where art takes on the investigation, analysis, critique, and expression of our humanity, the role of activism is to innovate, rebuild, and shift the way we engage in our social world.

Activism isn't just a social thing, but deeply personal. I don't see how I have any shot at creating the world I want to see if I am not first living as the person I want to be. Social activism has got to be connected to a strong life-practice in order to be effective. I ask myself daily "What are my values, where am I compromising them and why?" I also look for the environmental obstacles that prohibit me from becoming my best self. If society expects me to be compassionate, forgiving, and tolerant, I seek to find places in society that fill me up with enough loving resources to show generosity.

I think of love as emotional capital that comes from activities like play, fulfilling collaboration, and relationships. When the places and activities where I find this emotional capital is inaccessible or inadequate, it seems as though I am expected to simply alchemize generosity or compassion where there is only scarcity and and intolerance. Repositories for emotional capital, look like churches, museums, parks, collaborative work environments, and social connections within family— fellowship that allow me to form bonds with other people. When these are abundant, I have everything I need to do my work and collaborate.
I don't always see this in society sometimes when I do, there are unnecessary bureaucratic and social obstacles blocking access to these spaces and activities that seem counterproductive to a healthy society at large. In those moments I feel like it's my responsibility to speak up, not only for myself, but for those who might not have the ability or courage to speak up for themselves. The requisite for liberty is courage. Freedom is a constant struggle, critique is a form of loyalty, and justice is social health.

Justice is a product of the reclamation of our dignity, humanity, and integrity allowing us to be physically and emotionally healthy. There is nothing worth the compromise of our humanity. As I seek places and activities that remind me of my self-worth, love, and generosity I become more able to hold myself accountable to working toward the life I envision. This is real freedom—the resource and space to do the work to fulfill my potential. It might take some additional labor but it's worth it. You are worth it, I am worth it. Freedom is equal parts struggle and surrender.

When we talk about freedom it's not in isolation from every other thing in the world. There are very real obstacles like fear, and even external opposition. If you want to fly you're gonna have to address gravity! It's not all about fighting. Sometimes we have to be wise enough to let go of our predefined notions of what we are capable of. This can be as small as cutting loose on the dance floor or as big as quitting your job to follow your dreams. For me it was coming to terms with my definition of Manhood and confronting the limitations (and benefits) of holding onto ideas about how I think I should behave in society. Its different for everyone, but perhaps freedom isn't just about going with the flow, or about always battling convention, but instead, it's finding time and space to investigate what resonates as True, and being courageous enough to do what your spirit calls for.

Even though our concerns are imminent, the longest lasting solution might be one that begs a sustained effort. Start when you are ready and remain steady. This takes me back to self-care and discipline, but also being able to motivate myself when I am feel resistance to face the struggle that my own well-being requires. When I am having trouble getting motivated, the first thing I do is move my body. An object at rest wants to stay at rest, so the first thing is just start moving, anywhere, in any direction, to disrupt the stagnation. So I take a shower, make a sandwich, go for a walk, or clean the house. It's not all that different from activism. We have got to disrupt the status quo in order to create change. Sometimes the hardest part is getting started. It's not a cure-all but for me, it's a good first step. Before you march... walk.

Death.

Perhaps the biggest question I bump up against in my thinking is why any of this hardship is worth enduring in the first place. None of the wealth I accumulate will follow me to my grave, all of my relationships will eventually end, and every memory in my brain will fade away. Generally, I see other people address this problem in a few different ways: try and live as long as possible, do something that creates s legacy in its impact on the world after their death, or succumb to nihilism, realizing that everything is all temporary anyway. Personally, none of these strategies really help me make sense of the fact that death is always on my heels. Instead, I try to live deeply, fulfill my potential, and focus.

Attempting to live as long as possible doesn't really work because I'm gonna die anyway. Extending the length of my life doesn't inherently improve it's quality. If anything, it simply increases the number of positive memorable days and moments I have where I am learning, growing, and experiencing pleasure. Even then, at a certain point those same things that were once impactful to me decrease in impact, kind of like a tolerance builds up for the excitement of life. I feel like 90% of my life is pretty ordinary with spurts of amazingness 10% of the time.

There's not much I can do to expand my life much longer anyway beyond improving my health so if I were going to seek to expand, I would want to expand my capacity for experiencing life. Since time is relative to attention, I would also seek to get better at being more present in the existing amount of moments that I have. Living more deeply in the life I have gives me the chance to take the everyday moments that I experience between pivotal moments, and find something profound in them. I'd love to reverse the ratio to 90% profound moments and 10% mundane ones. By being more present, I work to cherish each breath a little more and push against seeing my everyday environment as ordinary. I don't have to live any longer, just appreciate the life I already have, more.

The other idea I challenge is the notion that I achieve some kind of vicarious immortality by doing work that creates a lasting impact. It may be true, and I don't think leaving a legacy is unimportant, but this projection of afterlife doesn't drive my actions while I'm alive. Instead, I think of my responsibility to the future to be stable ground from which to grow.

My life spans a period of time that is a part of the greater continuum of humanity, and a single drop in the flow of humanity doesn't have to create big ripples to be a part of a wave. I simply need to fulfill my potential here and now. Even though gaining influence can help me leave greater impact, I don't want to confuse my life goals with doing so. If my work is to be impactful, the process by which I gain influence should be as a result of doing and sharing it.

There's some risk that gaining influence for its own sake can become a distraction and pull me off course. I do what I can to honor my work, market it, and have it received by those who think it could be valuable to, but glory is not a motivator. **Let your work be fueled by vision, not ambition.**

Of all these existential traps, I am most prone to succumbing to nihilism. When I look around and see that everything is always changing, it can feel like seeking lasting impact is futile and it can make my work seem meaningless. It becomes difficult to understand why I would endure hardship for something that will eventually cease to exist.

One of the things that brings me back into engagement is realizing that, though change is constant, it doesn't happen without agents like myself working to enact that change. Secondly, I try to keep in mind that the kind of change that will come is yet to be determined and I have the opportunity to shape that change to be the most lasting. Thirdly, change is not the only constant. Both matter and energy are constants in the universe, and I am made of matter and energy. What I am experiencing as life is a concentrated period of change that has been brought into focus as a result of my sensory experience.

I try to remember that I have the opportunity to channel my attention to endeavors that I imbue with importance as a result of my focus on them. As long as I maintain enough clarity and alacrity to zoom in and out on things that I think are important, I have agency to choose what is important, and overcome the nihilism. It may be true that nothing is inherently meaningful, but it is my focus and care that allows me to create sense and meaning where there is none. Through subjectivity my experiences become as important as I decide they are, and this affects my experience of time, and value. Life for me is a journey that will inevitably end in death. No matter what, I am going to have good days and bad days, the only difference is that if I work at it, I get to have some input in what I see and do along the way.

I don't think of death as something negative that strips life away from me. I think of death as a well earned rest that follows a lifetime of having endured pain, struggle, and anxiety, and having indulged in joy, love, and play. A perfect life is one that is rich with experience, and allows me to recognize something universally true yet also unique to me. I want to leave it all on the field and die exhausted. The very thought of what to do with my life once caused me stress, because everywhere I looked people were telling me to pick one thing to define me and it never worked. What I want from life can't be summed up in a few words.

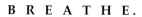

B R E A T H E.

Poem: I Want!

I want!
I wanna shake, I wanna jump, I wanna scream
I wanna fly, I wanna punch through the sky
I want to let the world know what to do with its limits.

I want a big ass theater with no one in it.
A galaxy of light just to practice in it
With the door unlocked so people can wander in it.

But life don't wait so I can't wait
The show is just rehearsal, all dressed
Like noone's waiting to be impressed
The study IS the test.

I wanna kiss, I wanna crow
I wanna grow but never grow up
I want a mini giraffe, I wanna make people laugh

I wanna smuggle dreams to life in bubbles
Always be in trouble
Double down on all bets
Trapeze with no net.

Swing, sing, brink, stay on the edge of
Death, I ain't afraid of.
Rest when I've had enough
Fuck, fight, film it.
Kill it on a beat.
Retreat, never look back. Only back flip
Bounce, pounce, give every ounce of soul
Soar, roar. I wanna roar. I wanna be a lion.
Die on stage. Tap with the feet of six centipedes.

Nothing can impede my progress,

My process is a step with each breath
And I'm blessed with lungs like thunder caves.

To jump is to fly, to fall is to live
To live is to give everything you ever got
To everyone who never had your chance.

Chance favors the prepared
Luck loves the paranoid.
I want a love that develops like a polaroid
Instantly. Infinitely vast
Like an infant naked in a bath
Splashing, giggling and laughing
Trusting.

Busting out of the dawn like the sun
That just couldn't wait to come up
And what I come up with
Is just the courage and wisdom to be all the man I can
And keep the little boy inside from being bored

So I plank, rap, dance with bright socks
To match a bright soul.
Sliding like ice, on hardwood floors
Along while angry neighbors rap on the door
Like they're asking for more.

I wanna mourn my mother properly.
Never hiding from the grief pain and sadness
Thankful that I even had the chance to have her for the
time that I did.

I wanna ball up on the floor like a little kid
And throw a tantrum, scream and cry
And curse God for taking her, thank God for making her

I want a hug, I want a kiss
I want to smell her fried chicken in the kitchen
I wanna hold my breath till I pass out,
Just to see if I could see her passby in the afterlife, I miss my
mother.

I wanna crash into the lips of a lover
Like a drunk driver, dizzy off optimism
Navigating by faith, propelled by hoverboard
I wanna hit the motherload.

Feed every starving artist
And build an apparatus that manufactures
Cash from creativity using advanced mathematics
I wanna make art, like air, free and refreshing
I wanna inspire, I wanna be fire or a firefly
I wanna skydive in the night sky and crash on the I-5

Just to stop people in their tracks for a second
Let them breath for a second, and learn to appreciate the seconds

I want, I want, I want
I want to speak five languages
Lounge in the laps of female strangers

I wanna transcend in dance until its all I do.
Walk. Dance. Breathe. Dance. Talk. Dance. Type. Dance

And I don't want to do it alone.
I want to hoist a baby up like Simba.

NANTS INGONYAMA BAGITHI BABA !

And run but naked though the jungle with a djembe beating my drum and chest

I wanna live in a big city with a small town feeling
I wanna parkour off buildings
And make a better system for how we raise our children
I wanna put everyone I've ever known in a room
And have them compare notes on how they've known me

I wanna fence in the Olympics, and make out backstage with a gymnast
I wanna bring home the gold
I wanna have a place that feels like home to go to

I'm just a lonely soul with lofty dreams and more space than he needs
And a handful of seeds.

I want to plan whatever will grow and let everyone know
There's no such thing as impossibility
All you gotta do is believe in your awesome.

I got a lot of causes to get lost in
And I don't know exactly how much I will accomplish
But for the first time
I know exactly what I want.

Instagram · March 21, 2017 · All the cool shit we post on social media only serves to perpetuate the myth of our assumed persona. There is danger in the conflation of performance with identity because they are not the same thing. But alas, the reality of the "attention economy" is such that social value is tied to relevance, and the sustainability of my livelihood is tied to my social value. For those of us creatives who choose to live a relatively public life or market ourselves via social media channels as freelancers or consultants, a part of our job becomes not "doing" or "making" but "appearing". It's important to recognize the difference between a job and a purpose. My job may be to appear but my purpose is to BE.

Facebook · March 19, 2017 · Rather than focusing on accumulating more technology and power to fit more and more tasks in a finite number of hours, I try making shorter To-Do lists. Focusing on what will be most impactful to my life and work gives me clarity. I seek to add value instead of hyper-productivity, but that's just me.

Twitter · April 29, 2017 · If it an idea is actionable... it's not a dream, it's a goal.

Twitter · June 12, 2016 · Every dream is a seed tended by the body, cultivated by the mind, that bears fruit to nourish the soul.

Facebook · June 21, 2015 ·
Don't feel guilty for being blessed, feel gratitude, and put that blessing to work for those who can't do for themselves.

ASK YOURSELF

How much of my time do I spend working for money vs. working on a passion project?

Do I feel a sense of purpose in my life? Is it connected to others or just myself?

If there was one skill or ability that would really excite me to learn, what would it be?

How much should I be paid to do what I love?

How much money is 'enough'for me?

What is a small business idea that is relatively interesting to me?

When was last time I celebrated my accomplishments?

What is something other people could learn from me?

Who are the 5 people who have impacted my life the most?

What would a perfect work day look like to me?

What local or global social issue, am I most concerned about?

Do I feel capable of accomplishing something great in my lifetime?

True or False:
When I sense something wrong/unethical going on, I speak up about it?

BUT ENOUGH ABOUT ME...

Curiosity Drive Model is a theory by George Lowenstien that says curiosity is an intellectual hunger, and that we move towards knowledge to fill the gaps of uncertainty in our life. I love this theory because it means that our appetite for knowledge is universal. Within this appetite though, our specific tastes are different, so we end up seeking out information that we crave intuitively.

I hope that sharing a bit about what my own path looks like, will inspire conversation for people in regard to their own beliefs, values, and interests. One of the first steps to finding your own path is getting in touch with what you are intuitively interested in. Curiosity is like a first kiss on your sixth sense. It tells you where to go and, gives you a hope and potential about how big a love could be if you accept the challenge to pursue it. **Hunger gives you a sense of direction.**

When you start the pursuit of quenching that mental hunger, you see more clearly what needs to be done to fulfill it. That hunger then turns into taste, the burning into discerning, and our curiosity becomes curation. You begin to be capable of qualifying those tastes and choosing to fulfill more complex cravings. It is like when we were babies, and we somehow developed the urge to walk. Eventually we were good enough that we could run and jump. It isn't until now when we are dancing, and sliding, and skating for leisure, that walking is something we do automatically, even though there was a time it was nearly impossible. We've already proven we have the capacity to change who we are and develop new skills that open our world to new experiences.

Once our horizons have been broadened, and we have a much more complex understanding of the world and ourselves, we then gain the ability to synthesize new ways of being and be creative in our life practice.

The most advanced uses of language include making up new ways to use language, like poetry, or even making up words that name thoughts and feelings. This pattern is not altogether different from life. We began very curious, and then put together ideas about what we want our life to be, based on previous notions. However, a really strong life practice is one where we are self-defining who we would like to be in the world, and working to realize that vision. The steps en route to bringing the vision to life is your path, your *Tao*. The way you move through the world should be as unique as how you sign your signature.

Along the way you'll meet people who will play large and small roles in your life. Some people are teachers, others are, lovers, collaborators, and some challenge us in was we don't always appreciate. Preparing to navigate these relationships comes from knowing your needs and boundaries; not just what you can or can't accept, but the limits of your capacity.

Within this is the paradigm of responsibility to care for yourself and also contribute. If you can accomplish both then you'll be of service to yourself and your community. Pay needs become clear and with that clarity a better understanding of the value of your work. When you are being forced to compromise or diminish that value, it is also important to have the courage to push against systems that are incomplete, imbalanced, or disfunctional, not only for yourself, but for those around you.

No one is an expert on this, and no one can plot the course for you. You'll definitely need help, but the journey is yours. Stumbling along the way is natural but if we have compassion for ourselves, it allows us to remove the expectation of living a "perfect" life in order to continue in the practice of life.

Sharing about how I live my life has brought me a lot of clarity and I hope that by reading my ideas, you are inspired to investigate your own ways of being and what is most important to you. When I get close to living up to the values and ideas I set forth in this book, it feels like I become more than just an artist, but a spirit embodied to fulfill a unique purpose, with a clear path to do so. And the results of fulfilling my own purpose have the potential to ripple through my relationships and effect greater change inspiring others to do the same.

Love, Maceo

Poem: Dynamite
I am a stick of dynamite, waiting to be lit.
My fuse is a short coil curl some may describe as nappy atop my head. Packed full of gun powder, I have seen my share of pain and joy.
I have travelled I have loved but I have yet to do what I was created to do.

Explode.
I sit in traffic, hoping to crash violently.
To be struck head on by another vehicle.
I hope for fire and metal and glass to burst out in all directions.
I want to go out with a bang.

It is the only eat I feel is fitting.
Cause sitting in this box is not living.
I only known one stick to light his own fuse, and he died at 33, but dynamite isn't supposed to last long.
It is supposed to leave a mark, create a space, move, or destroy.

It is passionate, I am passionate.
It is dangerous, I am dangerous.

I am a red stick of dynamite.
Black dynamite.
Boy Dynamite
Black boy dynamite.
I am a little black boy.

They tell me who I can be, and it scares me half to death.
They tell me about the change I can make and the power I have. How it's all up to me. "Just go and do it" " Reach for it" Take it" Grab it"

And I'm scared I've got them all fooled, scared of their disappointment and mine.
Because part of me believes them, cause I know there is something to this dynamic thing.
But what if I am a dud.
That lame popper whose biggest boom is his fuse.
You brace for the sound and then, it fails you.

I couldn't take being a dud, but I can't take this box either.
So I have to... I must... I will explode.
I was made to.
I can feel the chemicals in me and I can feel the respect I get. I am not unique but I am special.
I am dynamite. I am a bomb. I am the bomb.
I am the explosion.

I'm just waiting on my fuse to get lit.
Because when I become what I was made to become.
There will be a whole in a mountain.
Maybe not a big one, but I will knock loose a rock that hits a boulder and cause a landslide.
Move a city down a slope faster than a skier of a lift.
And you can't dodge a city.
You just become part of the movement.

And it doesn't matter how you feel about it.
The point is that you feel.
Explosions are undeniable, they stir up emotions, they cause chain reactions.
They inspire.

I am dynamite.
I was put here to make you feel.
I was put here to inspire.

ACKNOWLEDGMENTS

Art, science, and religion, all used to be the same thing. We didn't really have a word for it, but I suppose the closest translation would be "Life" but then we got good at evading predators, and we got good at finding and making food—so we had time on our hands. We used that time, to draw on caves, and stack rocks in intricate shapes, and stare up at the stars, make up stories, and separate these categories. I am just trying to follow the trail back to the pangea of human experience to see what truths run across all these fields. But since I am not really an expert in any of these areas I refer to a lot of people who know more than I do in each area, or are more intuitive or empathetic than I am. This book, along with the rest of my art practice, wouldn't exist without their influence.

Mom, Dad, and my brother Baron.
Whether it was my father's intellectual challenges, my mother's infinite love and wisdom, or my younger brother's acceptance, admiration and accountability, everything good about me arises when I am in the presence of any of them. Nothing could have prepared me for the loss of my mother, but I feel that in her own way, she did the work of providing me the tools to remember her well after her passing.

The Keelings.
Kimberly, Tonjua, Vanessa, Enid, Karen, Hope, Ampaw, and Ganny. Jonathan, Jason, Charlisa, Tiarra, Jeno, Inessa, Airami,Sunni, Aricca, Nia, Mikael, Amelia, Ayana, Aliyah and Monique. All those family days we had and reunions and laughs. You really were my first audience and first friends. I've never known a greater sense of community than what we shared.

The Currys.
Diane, Genie, Becky, Mateen, Bertha, Walter, Sharon, La-waun, Susan and Gino. Anthony, Malik, Kramo, David, Michael, Chanel, Carlos, Antwaun, Terrell, Geno, Devon-te, Shalia, Allen and Alene. I can't even begin to speak on what it has been like to have such a vault of love and understanding to draw from. To be embraced by your love and joy speaks to the power of love and its ability to connect us over miles and years.

Lorenzo Diggins Jr., Sundai Johnson, Ty Obscura.
As a creative team, to develop the collateral for the book, I could have chosen no one better. I hope we get to grow and work together more.

Ethan, Dan, Maggie, Audrey, Zion.
If it were not for our MOM sessions, and the bonds we shared individually, this project would have never come to life. Thank you for creating a safe space for me to be foolish, and ambitious, and vulnerable about my dreams and how to achieve them.

Natalie Patterson, Def Sound, Allison Kunath. There are no others I'd rather have around me to learn and grow with. As we've come to know each other and share in that process, I have received so much knowledge and love, wisdom, and support that I could never repay you or convey what an impact you have had on my journey.

Tracy Ann Essoglou, Kabira Stokes, Arianne Edmonds , Preston Smiles, Alexi Panos, Mathieu Young ,
Kiran Gandhi, Leila Jarman, Puno, Jet , Mandy Schuster, Danielle Leslie, Rene Perez, Chase Upton, Andrea Feyler, Chloe Iene Nadia Alvarez. You all are power houses that I don't get to see nearly as much as I should.

You inspire me and challenge me to be more like myself, and let me know what is possible when I do. Keep on keeping on.

Spaces:
Tuesday Verses.
Lorna Pickney, you were the first big sister I ever had and it makes me proud to see your legacy live on at the place where I first found my voice and confidence. Nickey Mc-Mullen, Casandra Broadusra, Megan Ricketts, Onaje Baldwin, Roscoe Burnems, Jamal Kelly and Veronica Evans ya'll were the first stage that acknowledged me as a writer and accepted me as a young brother.

Da Poetry Lounge.
Shihan Van Cliet, Brutha Gimel Hooper, Poetri, Dante Basco, the platform you have created has given so much to so many. It is where I was able to sharpen my own voice and reach towards my own version of mastery in a place I could feel respected and accepted. Yesika Salgado, Edwin Bodney, Danielle Bennett, Fiseha Moges, Joel Jaimes, Venessa Marco Carolyn Brennan, Vanessa Ayala,Mr. Poetic, Donny Jackson and Bird, what a fabulous cohort of writers I get to consider my alma mater.

Nelly Montenegro and Mr. Fish.
If it weren't for hanging at your place I don't know how the Tao Of Maceo would have taken shape but sitting in your backyard daydreaming was enough for me to unlock and clarify what I wanted to create.

Thank you for being the friends, family, inspiration and collaborators I needed, whether you knew it or not.

I can't wait to see what else we accomplish together.